101 Things Every Pastor Should Know

Jim Clark

101 Things Every Pastor Should Know
by Jim Clark

Printed in the United States of America

ISBN 1-594679-01-0

Unless otherwise indicated, Bible quotations are taken from the King James Version of the Bible.

www.xulonpress.com

Contents

Preface

In an age where knowledge abounds and education is a basic life accomplishment, many pastors still do not employ their skills successfully. In the days of old, a learned trade was passed down from a father to his son; this was known as *mentoring.* Today the art of mentoring is once again coming into vogue as an essential *key* in the learning process. This hands-on method, or one-on-one training, is being restored within the church.

The problem with many pastors is their lack of *confidence.* This lack induces fear, which in turn produces isolationism, which ultimately can result in either rejection or its opposite, a spirit of competition. Often the lack of self-confidence is caused by *pride:* a person is really too proud to admit he does not know how to be a pastor or do what is required of him. Like Adam, he tries to *hide* the fact and play the hypocrite, *acting* like he knows what he is doing. The antidote to all this is to repent, step out in humility, and start learning to be *transparent* (the hardest lesson I have ever attempted to learn in all my ministry). True transparency allows *relationships* to form, which in turn opens the door for effective mentoring to take place.

My purpose for sharing this book is to offer you a basic understanding of not just *how* to pastor, but how to have confidence that you are doing it right. From fifty years of experience—eighteen years as a pastor, eighteen years as a classroom teacher of pastors, and the last fourteen years as a *pastor of pastors* (mentoring)—I feel so blessed to share with you lessons learned from these many years. My prayer is that this book will give you a running start in what the Lord will take and bless for His glory and your excitement. It is simply fun to live out the "called" life.

This little book, *101 Things Every Pastor Should Know,* will help build your confidence as well as open your heart for the need of *mentoring.* And one day you will have the grand opportunity to mentor others. For mentoring not only quickens the harvest, but also better *conserves* the harvest.

This work is presented in a logical and sequential order; however, start where you see your immediate need lies and then continue to use it as a reference work for the many facets of the ministry you are called to do.

Please feel free to contact me for further needs you have or just to offer comment on the material.

1. Understanding the Fivefold Ministry

According to Paul, in Ephesians Chapter 4, Jesus gave *gifts to His church*, *ministry* gifts that are five in number: apostle, prophet, evangelist, pastor and teacher.

The apostle is mentioned *first* in every listing in Scripture. It is important to realize that the apostle (not one prophet, evangelist, pastor, or teacher) was the only ministry gift Jesus called and trained *before* the church was birthed in Acts 2. The reason for this is the character of the apostolic enabling: *vision, government,* and *order.* Tradition would have us to believe that apostles were men who were godly, holy miracle-workers. However, such are not apostolic giftings, but rather the responsibility of every Christian. Present-day ignorance of the *office* of an apostle is in direct proportion to the centuries of its absence.

We need to look again at early church history. With the ranks of the apostolic team refurbished in Acts 1, the first church went from 120 people in the morning of the first day to 3,120 by that afternoon. It grew to 8,120 people on the second day, so that in the first one-hundred-years-world, this percentage of growth set a record that has never been duplicated in all the rest of the 1900 years of church history. The reason is evident the God-ordained church planting program became extinct, as the office of apostle was done away with by the year 150 A.D.

Apostolic ministry teams planted, defined, disciplined, and encouraged the early churches, and they survived, even under traumatic persecution. Ninety percent of the churches started today have so little purpose and power and have so much confusion and disunity because they have no apostolic *foundation:* vision, government, and order (Ephesians 2:20).

The second ministry *gift* of the fivefold ministry is the prophet. The prophet is keenly aware of God's presence and revelation. He receives "words" from the Lord that help us to clarify and sharpen our purpose and vision. Often our ministry becomes tedious and heavy. A fresh word from God through the prophet lightens our hearts, deepens our resolve, and gives us fresh hope in our labors. His ministry is crucial *(foundational)* during the season of church planting, keeping the new work fresh and on track much the same as a sonogram does during the months of a pregnancy.

The third ministry *gift* mentioned is the evangelist. His gifting is best described as "panting" after the salvation of souls, be it an individual or the teeming masses of people. His spiritual DNA leaves him a poor candidate for shepherding and discipling the "sheep." Too often, both an evangelist and a congregation have suffered when he misdirects his gifting and attempts to pastor a local church.

The fourth ministry *gift* is that of the pastor. His giftings are quickly seen in his loyalty to his flock, his long-suffering for *each* sheep, and his unbending love for all his people. Because of his loyalty and compassion, he usually has difficulty with confrontation and heavy church discipline.

The fifth ministry *gift* is that of the teacher. The teacher is more gifted and suited in dealing with the truth of Scripture and doctrine than in dealing with people. To study Scripture, theology, and apology is his very joy. This searching out of the truth has opened the door for some within the ranks of teachers to lose their way and cross over into *error.* Know that almost every case of heresy was started by some *teacher.*

2. How Not to Wear Too Many Hats

The average pastor of a smaller church (without a staff) can come to the point of burnout if he spends too much of his time doing what he is not *called* and *gifted* to do. He must realize that he is neither gifted nor qualified—on purpose—to function in all of the *callings* of the fivefold ministry, even when it is obvious that all the callings are desperately needed. I spent too many years wasting too much time trying to do things *that I was not good at!* For example, I do not have the gifting of a prophet or an evangelist or a youth minister. I am a teacher. I knew instinctively by the Holy Spirit that these other office ministries were needed in my local church, but I had to learn the hard way that I could not effectively do them. I needed those who were called to do those things.

In most small churches, there is no provision for obtaining capable staff members who flow in the needed fivefold calling. You must find each of them and have these come alongside you to help you bring your local church to its rightful place in the Lord.

Within our fellowship of churches (International Network of Local Churches), we have a reservoir of the fivefold ministry giftings that move among our churches to help them achieve a full and needed balance of ministry.

The blessing of working together affords us the expertise that God intends for every local congregation, while releasing the *pastor* to do what he is supposed to do best.

3. Understanding Your Calling

First of all, there must be the undying conviction that you *are* called into the ministry of the Lord Jesus Christ. Poor results and rampant frustration within the ranks of ministry today decry the fact that many are in the ministry, but they were never *called* by God into the ministry. Like your salvation experience, the *call* is an experience that cannot be missed or denied; you will know and realize it. The ministry is not just another job where you train and then apply for a position. You do not choose to be in the ministry, nor should someone else push you into a ministerial *calling.* The *call* is solely initiated by God and is irrevocable. You may sin and thereby disqualify yourself from ministering, but God expects your immediate repentance, timely restoration, and your full reentry into your ministry calling.

The *call* is a life-changing, life-demanding, and self-surrendering experience that causes many to fear. However, the moment you surrender to the call of God on your life, great peace transcends your soul as you wait for the crashing wave(s) of God-given vision for your ministry.

If you are called, you can be sure that God has called you from the foundation of the world and has certainly put into you everything that will be required to do it. The calling may be covered with your "junk." Your gifting(s) may need to be set free through deliverance or need to be trained and cultivated, but they are resident within you. If you think that something is missing, know that God never included it for His plan in your life to start with.

Never self-limit yourself by the opinions of others, no matter what their stations in life may be. Just know that Jesus in you cannot fail. You not only contain gifting(s), but you are also required to invest them into the lives of others.

Take the time, regularly, to release and enhance your *calling*. This you do through prayer (and fasting), worshipping Jesus (coming into His presence to be with Him, not just for Him to bless you), diligent study (the Bible and other works), and last but not least, entering into a mentoring relationship with your "father" in the Lord or someone just like him.

Secondly, to ensure your success in your calling as a pastor, take on the mantle of Jesus and dedicate your life to *serving* people. It is essential that you have both authority and anointing because all your sheep will need your help—some more than others and some sooner than others—but all will need your servanthood. Should you run out of ideas or patience in serving, just reflect on how your mother lived for *you*.

4. Why Mentoring Is So Essential

What parenting is to family life, so *mentoring* is to ministry. It is very similar to the age-old practice of a father teaching his son (one-on-one) the family trade. Formal training for the ministry should hold an important place in your priorities, but without a mentoring process, you will soon find that formal training does not nor cannot impart the experience and wisdom that are so essential for ministry. There are only two ways to acquire the needed experience and wisdom: (1) to learn by trial and error (the hard way) or (2) to acquire them both from someone who has them—a mentor.

It is here that most men entering into the ministry make a serious mistake. Starting off with a good measure of insecurity, they assume the naive idea that being leaders, they are supposed to have an answer or an idea for every situation and that they are responsible to do everything there is to do. With their insecurities well in place, pride requires them to isolate themselves from any outside help, particularly from other ministers. As isolation grows, so do the spirits of competition, mistrust, and suspicion towards all other ministries. Finally, when such men come to the end of themselves and timidly begin to seek help, they have real difficulty finding someone whom they can trust. Know that entering into a mentoring relationship early in your ministry will stop all this foolish, pride-caused trouble from happening.

Mentoring is accomplished only by the building of relationships. True relationships happen only when we learn to become *transparent.* Being transparent is one of the most difficult things—if not the hardest—for most men to do. Building relationships takes time, time to demonstrate love and build trust. But it is only here that mentoring can do its best job. Relationships afford knowledge and wisdom; answers come and solutions happen. Mentoring releases the minister to enter the next level of his calling, each time and on time.

Mentoring works best one-on-one or through small group meetings. Pastors meet within a certain geographical area, and someone with an apostolic calling mentors the group through a living example and with pertinent and meaningful instruction. This time together allows for plenty of time for dialogue. In this way, each minister gleans and/or shares something useful during the session. In these times, he gains new confidence with his mentor, with his peers, and within himself. I have seen it many times, watching a group of pastors grow from being independent, self-conscious, and awkward spectators into becoming friends who can relate to and trust one another. They begin to open up to one another personally and then to share their giftings in one another's local churches. When these types of relationships are forged, nothing can stop a corporate vision from readily being accomplished.

Mentoring provides much fruit. It guides you into greater character, including ethics as well as self-assurance. Mentoring helps you to discover and achieve all your God-given giftings, your calling, your vision, and strategies. Mentoring affords wise counsel that can eliminate costly mistakes in judgment and procedure. True mentoring places you and your ministry in a place of accountability so necessary for proper, honest stewardship.

With the *arrival* of the apostolic ministry back into the church, mentoring can now assume its rightful and needful place within our lives. Now for the first time in centuries, the *sons* of God in the ministry have access to *fathers* within the ministry. We are seeing the role of the apostle taking its scriptural place. The apostles are not only those whose hearts are inspired with the vision of church planting and church maintenance, but also those whose lives, ethics, wisdom, order, and counsel publicly afford them their lead place in ministry (this is why the Scriptures list the *apostle* first in every listing, without exception). This *lead* position places them into the church *governmentally* (government in every realm is really applied spiritual authority). As fathers, they are able and willing to follow Jesus' example, who is the *chief* apostle (Hebrews 3:1).

5. How to Discern the Perfect Will of God

To know the Lord is the meaning of all life. God has a purpose for each one He brings into His world. His purpose for me is really *His* will, not His will for *me.* The moment I inject *self* into the picture, I distort God's will with selfish prejudice. God has a will that includes me and that inclusion is all about me, but it is not *for* me—it is *for* Him! Until we remove self from our thinking, we are in constant danger of imposing upon or altercating (polluting) God's purpose for our lives.

It is necessary to know that God's will is just one will that operates in two realms: *perfect* and *permissive.* For example, you can be in God's perfect will by tithing and simultaneously stay in His permissive will by holding an offense. It is your God-given responsibility to, in time, bring every area of your lifestyle into the perfect will of God.

To enable you to enter into God's will, He first gives you the *revelation* of His will. Then you must make the *decision* to obey that revelation. Proof of this being done is His *peace* that maintains your life moment by moment.

Next comes the time of your *preparation,* which should precede your *separation* into your ministry. Many become frustrated when through immaturity, they reverse this order.

Still harder is the discerning between the happenings in your life as to whether they are *providential* or *circumstantial.* Providence is a provision of the Lord, but circumstances are factors (natural or spiritual) that do not promote God's will or may, in fact, hinder you. A combination lock has many potential settings, but only the right three numbers in the correct order and direction will open the lock. Know that you can overcome circumstances, but you should flow with providence. Further clarification: The providence of God allows trials, but circumstances are often temptations from the devil. Through *wisdom,* providence directs you, but circumstances bring confusion. Through the *Scriptures,* providence lines up with the Bible, but circumstances have the tendency to ignore or offend Scripture. To make *identification,* what is providence to one may be a circumstance to others (e.g., Jonah and the sailors on the boat to Tarshish).

God's will always happens in this prescribed order: *general* then *specific.* God's general will is for all people (e.g., the Ten Commandments), but His specific will pertains to you, right now (e.g., your call to preach the Gospel). If, however, you are not doing God's general will, you cannot be eligible for further revelation of His specific will.

In receiving God's specific will, five factors must be considered: (1) Timing—Is this the correct time to be doing it? God always had in mind a king for Israel, but the people of Israel got ahead of themselves when they demanded Saul. (2) Attitude—If your heart is not pure, you cannot handle God's will. He will keep you in a state of minor crises until you get your heart right. (3) Place—Your ultimate vision may include a megachurch, but you will need to work your way up into that place, even as David did in becoming king of all Israel. (4) Way—It cannot be God's will when you do a right thing in a wrong way, such as pastoring a church and putting your ministry before your family. (5) Person—You see the vision, but you are not the one to accomplish it all. When God told me to plant the last church I pastored, he gave me a goodly vision of the work. After ten years of labor, we were not close to achieving what I first saw in the vision. I whined to the Lord one day, complaining about this. He immediately spoke to me and said it would be done, but not all by me, rather by my son. In a state of selfishness, I took His word to mean that I would soon die and be out of the way. I became very humble and repented; then He told me that soon I would be moving in a new direction of His will. Whew!

One further word on God's will: I call it the principle of Ziklag. While at Ziklag (2 Samuel 27:6), King David thought it to be the lowest hour of his career. But in remaining humble, faithful, and true to his vision, he finally became king while at Ziklag. Remember, too, that faithful Joseph was catapulted from prison to prime minister of Egypt, fulfilling God's dreams to him. You must keep your heart right, even when it seems like your lowest hour, for it is here the next event in God's will happens.

6. Setting the Ministerial Priorities of Your Calling

Many in ministry with the call of God on their lives make unbiblical decisions about the priorities of their callings. In the zest and fervor of the call of God on their lives, they go all out for God and make the mistake of confusing their relationship with God with their ministry for Him. They are *not* the same.

God always and in everything must have top priority within your life. It is to Him you owe your unswerving dedication, loyal service, and unceasing love. On the other hand, your ministry, or calling, is not your relationship with God; it is your service to God's people. No matter what your giftings or calling may be, your work for God is not the same as your relationship and worship to God.

The Lord Jesus Christ is without question your first priority in life, called or not called. Your second priority of calling should be your immediate family: wife, children, and parents—and in that order. The pressures of ministry and the tremendous demands it makes on your life cannot be confused with your responsibility to your family. All too often we find the family of the minister being neglected because of the unceasing demands of ministry. To be guilty here (and most are) is to sin because of wrong priorities. The husband and wife, according to God's plan, are *one.* Those in the ministry are no exception. Your ministry is not holier or better than your relationship with your wife and children. They come before everyone else under your charge.

This responsibility is not limited just to divine order in the home, although it includes it. Your wife is the balance to your call in ministry, no matter how public her role may be. The needs of your family—spiritually, emotionally, physically—must stay prioritized above everyone else within the jurisdiction of your ministry. As you make your family your second priority, your ministry will be released to a new level, both personally and publicly.

Your work for God must remain third place in your priorities of life. All too often a costly mistake is made at this point. The minister is tempted to set his ministry priority too high, as discussed above, or too low. Let me explain what I mean by too low. If your ministry is your *job,* then you treat it like the world treats a career. Prestige, power, or remuneration become goals in place of God's will or people (lost and saved alike).

Telltale signs that your ministry is in the wrong priority slot include the following: (1) professionalism, the skilled application of your ministry gifts with selfishness or insincerity (just ask three people in your congregation that are not personal friends, or better yet counted as enemies, about this); (2) secularism, a carnal lifestyle revealed by what your mind normally runs to, what your topic of conversation usually drifts to, and what your favorite pastime is (sports, politics, finances, hobbies, etc.); and (3) lack of vision, as you plod along each day, just following a routine and doing what needs to be done. Your ministry has become little more than rote and routine. There is no plan, no vision—just the "same-o, same-o." I call this failing faith.

Set your priorities according to the principles of God's Word. Jesus Christ is first, without exception, always before task and time. Make the love of your natural life, God's gift of family, second only to the Lord Himself. Endeavor, thirdly, to make your calling and/or ministry the greatest gift to the world it can be, for Jesus' sake.

7. How to Set the Pastor's Salary

The first thing you need to understand in setting the pastor's salary is realizing whose responsibility it is to do so. First, the pastor should objectively know his financial requirements and accurately set them down. Secondly, his apostolic presbyters should look over his budget (salary needs) and give an experienced assessment of this salary proposal (I do this on a regular basis). Thirdly, the pastor should meet with his local church leadership for a confirmation of this budget item.

Many men are uncomfortable in dealing with their own salaries, but they have no need to be since they are accountable to their apostolic oversight. Some men of God, being new at all this (most adults do not have nor have ever made a real budget and lived by it), find themselves in a quandary as to how to set their salaries at all. It is time for you to learn and set a good example of stewardship before your people; your apostolic father can assist you in setting up your personal budget (salary).

You must realize that most church members want their pastor to make a good living. I have discovered through the years that a novice pastor usually tends to underpay himself, wrongly placing the ministry in a higher priority than his family, placing undue hardship on his family and often becoming an embarrassment to his church family as well.

Remember: There is only so much money available, so proper prioritizing of the church budget is essential (we will discuss church finances in a later section). The tendency of the novice pastor as the visionary leader is to be the last to be paid, and when there isn't enough money to go around for the month, he takes the hit for the next month or so. This need not happen if a proper budget is in place. It is wise to walk in the counsel of your apostolic covering so things like this do not happen.

The apostolic covering can introduce you to the many sources which have expertise in church finances that can help you take proper advantage of authorized expenditures allowed by the government to be exempt from taxation (there are numerous expenses within household and ministry, but the rules change regularly). This portion of the pastor's salary is not included in his taxable salary (W-2 form) and will actually increase his take-home salary.

Remember: If you are having problems with your personal finances, you will without a doubt have problems with the church's finances. I have found from proven experience that many times you do not really need more money. Often what you really need is more and better *stewardship.* Learn well this rule: God will never give you more money than you are <u>being</u> a good steward over.

8. How to Effectively Practice the Sabbath Rest

If a pastor has a problem with any of the Ten Commandments, it is probably with keeping the fourth commandment. This is not because it is vague or difficult to understand; its clarity is obvious. The problem arises from our culture. *Pragmatism* has invaded even the most spiritual inner sanctums of our lives. In our blurring of what is secular and spiritual, both have lost their true identity to us.

The Lord states very clearly that six days in the week are for work. Our culture has weaned the workweek down to four ten-hour days, leaving us three days for pursuing leisure. The quest for less work time has not been raised so much out of laziness, but rather from the lack of true understanding of God's purpose for work and man's created privilege in it, which is to take rightful pride in his created giftings and skills with which to serve mankind and honor God.

Because we have missed God's purpose for our working, we have totally lost the purpose of our need of rest (Sabbath). On which day we rest is not as theologically important as the sequence of the days: one in seven. Since the New Testament indicates that we are to maintain public, congregational worship on the "first day," or the "eighth day," and since this public worship is the highest diversion to our daily work, Sunday is the most profitable day for us to rest (Sabbath).

Again, rest is not to be confused with leisure. Our culture has substituted leisure for rest. Know that what cotton candy is to your stomach, leisure is to your spirit and soul: little of nothing! God did not command you to be involved in a diversion (leisure) from work, but to rest from your six days of work.

With your cessation from your work, you can and should *evaluate* your work: Whom do I really work for? Why do I do this work? How well was it done? What was it worth? Secondly, you should *recalibrate* your work ethic and spiritual values that have been bombarded, bruised, or eroded while combating the secular world all during the workweek. Thirdly, you have a peaceful time to *contemplate* how your true life's mission (purpose) is coming along. These things can be inspired during your time of public worship, if not accomplished at that time. What you do physically or "fun wise" is not the issue here; the issue is whether or not you are following God's commandment and have your life priorities straight.

Since most in ministry work their hardest on Sundays, when and how do they rest? The answer lies in the sequence (one in seven) of days. As a pastor, you must, with jealous determination, set aside a time (hopefully a day) that you can devote to evaluation, recalibration, and contemplation.

9. How to Start/Plant a Local Church

The only example of kingdom expansion given in the book of Acts is through *church planting;* evangelism through crusades, outreaches, or other means was not the norm as exampled by Paul and other apostolic teams moving about the known world. Paul went into towns and cities with one Spirit-led strategy, and that was to plant New Testament churches. It is high time that our churches today return to this singular, successful pattern (within the first hundred years the Gospel was established in every part of the civilized world through church planting) and see their monies and efforts directed to a permanent and exponential harvest of souls through church planting.

There are two ways to plant a church: (1) You can release a sector of your cells (small groups) within a certain geographical area of your city, along with the main leader of that sector, and start a new church plant. This can be done quite easily and economically, and it is quite obvious that in a given time, your entire town would have viable new churches and then with geometric progression move into new, unchurched communities. (2) Several churches can come together and provide a church-planting team, along with the necessary finances, to be trained and equipped by apostolic ministry for church planting and then to be sent out to the chosen locality.

In facilitating the first method, several things need to be observed in preparation for the planting of a new church and is best undertaken with the *office* of the apostle present or available. First of all, the morale and financial strength of the *sending* church must be monitored so as not to thwart the momentum of its local operation. The *going* church must be under apostolic supervision until its leadership and finances are stable. It will relate governmentally as a daughter church until it is strong enough to become a self-sufficient work. This new plant will be in covenant with the sending church to provide 10 percent of its income for other apostolic church plantings and 10 percent for regular missions endeavors as it becomes a sister church.

The second method will also need the presence of apostolic ministry, both to select the appropriate place for the plant and to ensure the success of this endeavor, because many aspects of church government will have to be initiated and set in place. There first must be an apostolic church (one that has apostolic vision and apostolic presence within) to host the team preparing for the new church plant. The ministry team can be assembled from various sister churches that are ready to release proper (proven within their local church) ministry and to assume the financial responsibility for the new church plant. Obviously, some of the team will go permanently (the pastor and/or other fivefold ministry), and some of the team may go only temporarily (six months to a year) to assist with their giftings in helping establish the new church.

In every case, the church-planting team is under apostolic supervision to ensure that as a team they are compatible and committed to the vision and to one another. This may take several months. During this preparation time together, they will grow in vision and understanding of the strategy, as well as in their specific roles in the new church plant. It must be decided who, if any, will have to obtain secular work to live, and how long each temporary worker will stay. The team should be led by the apostolic ministry to visit and sound out the new church site at least once before the team goes out permanently. When the departure time arrives, each participating church will come together to celebrate in a combined "sending" service, pledging afresh their financial commitment to the new venture. It will be the apostolic ministry that will supervise and coordinate the new church plant to keep the sending churches well informed with responsible reports.

There will come a time for releasing the mission church plant and recognizing both spiritually and legally that it has become a sister church; that is, one that is assuming its responsibility for its autonomy of vision and financial independence and is now ready for an equal place within the fellowship of churches from which it began. This timing will be determined by the apostolic ministry.

A "setting in" service should now take place at the new church plant location. The new pastor and his wife will receive the laying on of hands in a public service that sets them in officially as the visionaries in charge of that local work. This ministry will be done by the new pastor's apostolic presbytery (consisting of his pastor, the apostle supervising the church plant, and at least one other apostolic minister making up the apostolic oversight to which he is personally accountable).

At the next gathering of the fellowship of local churches, this new pastor and church will be recognized and received into fellowship. This procedure is very much like a child being born into a family.

10. The Apostle's Role in a Church Plant

If there is one place in which the office of the apostle is basic, the testimony of the book of Acts makes it clear that it is in church planting, *the* fundamental tool of kingdom expansion and world evangelism. The nature of apostolic ministry is found within its name: "sent forth one," the assured connection through the relationship of the One Sending and the ones being sent. It is this relationship within the office of the apostle that carries out the purpose of God with His authority and order. That purpose is *church planting.*

Paul referred to the ministry of the apostle as "a wise masterbuilder" (1 Corinthians 3:10). In the same verse, he also talked about his work as laying "the foundation"; it is concluded that apostolic work is initial and fundamental to God's great plan to spread the Gospel, receive the harvest, and maintain the harvesters by planting local New Testament churches all over the world.

Within the apostolic DNA is the gifting of *government.* Government (like a train runs on two tracks) moves in authority and order; true authority bespeaks of God's holy will, and divine order signals His righteous works. These two attributes release within the apostolic ministry the discernment, vision, courage, and compassion necessary to penetrate a natural and cosmopolitan society in order to plant a visible expression of the presence of God: a local church.

Within the ministry is the ability to recognize other fivefold ministries and their part on the church-planting team, unfold spiritual strategies for church planting, and anticipate and disarm the devil. The apostle's calling also moves with great wisdom, not only gleaned from experience, but also divinely inspired (why seemingly young men can flow in the calling).

11. How to Finance a Church Plant

There are two things that basically hinder the furtherance of the Gospel: *ignorance of the Word of God* and *money.* At this point in my ministry, I do not know which one is the greater hindrance. Surely the lack of finances is formidable; there are usually people who are led to do the work, and certainly the need is ever present and the timing easily discerned, but the need for finances ever blocks the vision for further ministry.

I have discovered through the years of ministry that we do not always need more money, but we usually need better stewardship of the money we are presently responsible for. I have also noticed another problem: that some mistakenly perceive that ministry is an automatically salaried position. The truth of the matter is that those of us in ministry <u>must</u> minister, whether we are paid for it or not! There is built within the heart of everyone called into ministry a definite sense of stewardship and sacrifice. There must be a balance between "where there is a will, there is a way" and a plan for responsible financial provision and accountability.

The matter of first financial concern in starting a church plant is that the sending church(es) retains a strong and sufficient financial base, for if the sending church becomes too weak financially, it places in jeopardy not only the new work, but also the entire vision of the sending church. The cost must be counted before the church plant is started.

The financial base of the church plant must be correlated with the help the sending church commits to, along with the projected income of the new church, to ensure that adequate funds are available. A budget (progressive) is developed before the work begins. The budget will decree the priorities of the beginning ministry. Will the lead man (pastor) receive money? Will he have to take a secular job? Will it be full-time or part-time? Will it be necessary to start with a facility, or will the ministry begin in a home or some other borrowed facility (building rent or a building note in the immediate future must be placed within the progressive budget)? Will utilities be a factor and to what amount? How much equipment and supplies (furniture, sound, administrative) will be donated, and how much will have to be purchased? Parking must always be considered.

One financial decision that must be in place as the church plant begins is the new church's financial responsibility for investing in something bigger and outside of itself (just like the personal tithe). Conviction and wisdom decree that the church plant be financially responsible to begin immediately sowing money back to the sending apostolic church, not to pay back any monies given, but to join in the vision and responsibility to see other churches planted. Our fellowship of churches (International Network of Local Churches) advises 10 percent of the gross income of the church plant be designated for this. We further recommend another 10 percent be given to world missions, right from the inception of the new work. This instills within the church plant the reality of Jesus' Great Commission, as well as develops a giving spirit within the people, thus opening the door for God's blessings to flow upon the vision of the house and upon the people personally.

12. How to Choose and Train a Team for a Church Plant

Each local church is responsible for teaching, encouraging, and then recognizing fivefold ministers within the body of Christ as they rise up within the leadership of the church. There should be a plan not only to recognize those called into fivefold ministry, but also to establish a means to provide selective, essential training to equip them and encourage them as they prepare themselves to serve the Lord in a full-time capacity.

Whether your church is cell-based or program-based, there is a common telltale sign for recognizing the called as they rise up within the local body. It is wise to realize that many times they themselves do not recognize what God is doing in their lives (young Samuel had to be instructed by Eli to recognize and surrender to the call of God on his life). Those that are called usually become frustrated, wanting to do more but usually not knowing *what more* to do. Even when they are given *more to do,* it does not satisfy their souls because the God-given challenge and direction on their lives cannot be fulfilled by unrelated or routine responsibilities (this is not unlike Adam's frustration of being lonely in the Garden but not knowing what his problem was until the Lord told him to seek for a mate).

As their pastor, you need to be spiritually aware of this and to have your leadership report to you when a normally faithful member becomes frustrated with his consecration or becomes bored to the point of rebellion over assigned tasks. As an apostle, I call aside these chosen few to meet with me on a Saturday morning. No room for false expectations is given, except that they may learn how to increase their joy and effectiveness in serving the Lord.

Apostolic gifting includes the recognition of fivefold ministry and usually anticipates their calling, often before they do. During the discussion, I share the meaning of fivefold ministry, along with the explanation and place of vision within ministry. Then I have each one write out a short expression of his heart's desire: "how I see myself serving the Lord." This, along with the report of the leaders and the pastor, allows for pinpointing with a high degree of accuracy any calling, if there is one, on each person's life. Often there will be those that are vague about it, which gives indication that there is no real call upon their lives of yet; these are just returned to their normal duties without feeling any sense of failure.

Those with every indication of a call upon their lives receive further counsel and are then challenged to enroll in an in-house curriculum for ministry training. When their hearts bear witness to the call upon their lives (prophetic confirmation helps with this), it should be announced publicly in a worship service. From this pool of ministerial resources, a church-planting team can be put together.

A new church plant will also need helps ministries, those who are not called into the fivefold ministry but have giftings and are willing to launch out and help on a part-time basis (just like all church members normally should). The team can use musicians, street evangelists, children's workers—really, the list is unlimited. Usually these people will be assigned to the new church plant for a short term of service (a commitment for a specific time is essential), unless later they are led to remain permanently with the new church.

The announcement has already been made to the fellowship of churches, or sister churches, by the sending (apostolic) church that a new church is to be planted in a certain area. All volunteers are interviewed. Sister churches are now asked to screen and lend others who are needed for this church plant (both called and lay ministry). With the team selected and the financial arrangements settled, a visit to the site for familiarization and a prayer walk will next be done to inspire vision, lend perspective, and promote enthusiasm.

The sending church will host the team as they spend time getting ready, ensuring that leadership, order, and relationships are solidly intact. When the target date arrives, all the sending churches gather together and publicly send out the team.

13. How to Know When the Church Plant Has Autonomous Vision

From the day of inception, the church plant will be monitored and mentored by apostolic ministry, not only to ensure that the daily functions are properly and adequately carried out and that the vision is on schedule and is continuing correctly, but also to ascertain when the *vision of the house* becomes visibly maintained by the new pastor and sustained by the new church. It is at this point that the new church transitions from a daughter (mission) church and becomes a sister church within their fellowship of churches. This is very much like having a child leave the home to become married.

The new pastor will be doctrinally and philosophically the same as the planting church(es), but he will have his own identity and gifting that will be shaped by his calling and the pursuit of his vision. Again, like in marriage, a son will follow all the rules and protocol of marrying a bride, but he picks his own bride. So is the vision of the house (specific to that ministry) birthed. The pastor's style, gifts, and spiritual direction will formulate a distinctive role to fulfill God's plan for that community/area.

All churches are singular in purpose—the Great Commission—but their (each) vision of the house provides a kaleidoscope of functions. Just as a community needs a police department, a fire department, a city council, a post office, etc., with each fulfilling its specific function within the community, so should the various churches within a community/area serve the common cause, each having its own functional purpose and ability (large and small, worship, street ministry, TV ministry, etc.) without independent duplication, which wastes money and fosters confusion and competition.

Vision is realized and pursued best in the context of a mentoring relationship (apostolic). It is a serious mistake to release a pastor and a new church plant prematurely; that is, before the vision of the house is operating effectively, very much the same as it would be a tragedy to let your child get married when he or she was only eleven years old. *Vision* is the valid criteria for becoming a responsible ministry in proper place within the community. It is quite obvious that there are too many established, indigenous churches in existence where the pastor does not have or function within his vision; let us not add to this confusion.

Vision is to a church what a *destination* is to a trip. Many in ministry are just driving but have no idea where they are going. Others in ministry are driving, but on a racetrack. Every day is the same for them; all they do is make *another lap*. Each morning they get up and do whatever is crying the loudest for their attention and never get on with the goals God has given them to do. If you are not sure where you are going and don't have a plan (strategy) to get there, you won't.

Another aspect of vision: It has to be communicated to the people, or you will find yourself going on alone and will wind up complaining about the lack of committed help from your people. It is next to impossible to follow you if you are not sure where you are going and why. Many pastors think they are good communicators because they preach well, but in all reality, their communication stops there. Some pastors fail to regularly inform, exhort, and update the church of the vision of the house, and many others have little or no vision to communicate. A pastor without a vision is as irresponsible as is the sea captain of a fully loaded vessel leaving port without a destination.

When apostolic ministry verifies the presence and clarity of the new pastor's vision of the house (the vision should be written out in a clear, succinct form and exhorted publicly on a regular basis) and verifies the functional success of the vision of the house (the people are generously supporting and following it with enthusiasm), the church plant is then capable of both reasonable growth and reproduction; it can now be recognized as a regular sister church within the fellowship of churches.

14. How to Get Vision

Vision is the awareness of God's *purpose* for your life ministry. God is a God of purpose (reason, cause, plan, and strategy). Nothing has or will ever be done by God without purpose. He made each of us *on* purpose and *for* a purpose. It is our individual responsibility to seek, and it is the Holy Spirit's job to inform us of, our God-assigned purpose for life.

When someone is called into fivefold ministry, God reveals, confirms, and enacts within the person's spirit the vision He has for him and the person's service to Him (ministry). Like a child that never attends school, he may be very intelligent, but he lacks knowledge; so it is with our calling when we do not submit to its priority in our life (vision). Even Jesus had to grow in knowledge and wisdom because of His humanity; so we must be ready and willing to follow the vision God has planted in our heart and grow in its understanding. Those who feel aimless or fruitless in life are not lacking talent or opportunity; their destiny becomes frustrated by not recognizing their purpose (vision) in life.

The call upon your life is the "official" track upon which it will run its race. The vision must be discovered, just like the talent to play the piano. It must first be discovered and then practiced daily. Again, like playing a piano, you start with very simple tunes, and as you progress, your music becomes more intricate and involved. So it is with vision and ministry. To keep the analogy going, you would be wasting time to take a piano lesson and then practice all week long on a tuba; yet many that are called wind up doing just this. There are teachers who should be on the mission field, pastors who are called to be evangelists or prophets, those in the ministry who were never called, and many, many who are called but will not submit to it.

When I was called, I knew how to do nothing. The only thing I did know was that God had a purpose for my life, and I was relentless in trying to find it. Slowly, step by step, it became clear. I knew I was God's for Him to do with as He willed, and I was as determined as a Louisiana mosquito to find it and do it! The more I prayed and served, the clearer it became: I was to be full-time. I was to teach. I was to put in and keep in order the work of the ministry (my whole system reeked with order and government from my earliest memory and all through my military service prior to entering into the ministry). It turned out to be a long journey, and much of the territory I passed through was unfamiliar; but in His timing, I arrived at the home base of my calling: doing the work of an apostle. It's like a singer: He doesn't need an opera house to sing in; he sings in the shower, he sings on the street, he sings everywhere he goes. He just sings!

Now concerning you and your vision, you were called to fulfill your purpose in God. With the call comes the vision. What do you see yourself doing? What do you do best that is God-honoring? What do you like to do? What is the very burden of your heart? When you finally saw your wife, your personal life's destiny was fixed; so it is with your vision.

Then write your vision down. Seek confirmation of it through *your* pastor. Stand by, for somewhere along the way the prophet will also bring clear confirmation. As you write it down, begin to make it clear and brief; it now becomes the *slogan* for your life. It becomes a passion; it is all you see and want to talk about. Now it is time to let the Spirit of God give you the strategy (method) to make your *dream* become reality.

Your *vision* has arrived. You know who you are and what God's purpose is for your life. As Paul explained, we all have our specific lane on the track in the race of life; others are also running, but you are running the race that God has set before you. With this vision, you now have direction and are equipped to lead your ministry.

Just a word about what vision is not: Vision is more than a strategy or a method or even a plan. God anoints vision; it is through vision that the anointing comes upon the plan, strategy, or method. This is why you can go to a conference and learn about someone else's successful strategy and hurry home to try this fantastic idea, only to find that it does not work. When you just copy someone else's plan, method, or strategy without having the vision, there is no anointing; it is like trying to bake a cake in a cold oven. It worked for him because it was *his* vision that provided the anointing upon the strategy that gave him the blessed results.

There are no anointed strategies or methods outside of a God-given vision. Do not start your ministry based upon a popular strategy, but rather begin your ministry with God-given vision that is based upon your God-given purpose in life.

15. How to Distinguish Vision from Strategies, Plans, and Methods

Vision comes from God and has to do with *purpose*. It is greater than what you do or how you are to do something. Vision is the announcement of *why* you live; it portrays your destiny in life. Vision is a passion that does not pale. Strategies, plans, and methods come and go; vision is indelible. Vision is like a craftsman, and the strategies, plans, and methods are just the tools in his hand. The craftsman's tools wear out and are replaced. A strategy, plan, or method without vision is like a borrowed tool; it does not make you a craftsman.

Strategies, plans, and methods are rarely anointed outside of God-given vision. By themselves, they are no more effective than your recording of a $500 deposit into your checkbook without actually making the deposit. It just generates confusion.

On the other hand, if someone just rambles on about a so-called vision but never accomplishes anything, he is either deceived or lazy. God never awards vision without adequate strategy and passion to accomplish it.

Vision is personal and subject to the will of God. God's will always has a proper time, place, and person and cannot be delegated; on the other hand, strategies are always impersonal and can be delegated. Vision is like the horizon, ever in front of you, but never reached; strategy is like the vehicle that carries you toward the horizon. If you can fulfill your vision within your lifetime, then it is not your vision; it is simply a task (step) within your vision.

16. The Vision and Your Staff

The set man of the local church (usually a pastor, but sometimes another one of the fivefold ministry) carries the *vision of the house.* The vision is the purpose that God has for a local church (ministry) in a certain area given to the set man along with his unique giftings.

This vision of the house is uniquely given to each set man of the local church (ministry). It is the set man's responsibility to communicate this vision to all the church, especially to the leadership, and to see that it stays on track within the given timetable of the Lord.

The pastoral team and all the membership are obligated to know and follow the vision of the house. There is no place for alternative visions within that local work, for this always proves to be divisive and confusing, a common problem in local churches.

In the course of time, it is normal for a staff member to receive from the Lord a vision of his own. When this happens, the staff member must be released and properly sent out to pursue his (new) vision. He will be given adequate help and offered a continuing relationship between the two *sister* ministries. I regularly reviewed with my staff the principle of "one house, one vision" and stated how the time would come when each potential set man would receive his own vision.

A leadership problem will arise when a staff member changes vision (often not even realizing it). When this happens, he usually thinks it is the senior pastor who has changed visions, or worse, that the pastor has become unfaithful to the vision of the house. This losing the vision always ends up in some act or attitude of rebellion if not discovered and dealt with quickly. It is essential for every senior pastor to be aware of this possibility and to be ready to deal with it. In our staff meetings, I always reviewed the vision and correlated it to our weekly operation to check the faithfulness of the team to the vision of the house. The moment I discovered someone moving away from the vision, I took him aside and clarified it and then showed him where he was missing the vision of the house. If he could not get back on track, I asked him to prepare to leave so that he could openly follow his (new) vision. You cannot travel on two roads at the same time.

17. How to Communicate Vision

Vision cannot be delegated, any more than I can delegate my place as husband to my wife to another. The strategies pertaining to the vision can be and must be delegated; thus, it is imperative that everyone in the local church (ministry) understand the vision of the house, clearly and completely. Comprehensive communication of the vision is essential.

A common problem within leadership is the failing to adequately communicate *all* the facts pertaining to vision. We see it all in our minds and in our enthusiasm just fail to communicate it all (a common weakness), then get upset when others know only portions (just what we said) of the vision. Counselors face this dilemma perpetually as they deal with marriage and church problems. Too often pastors assume (wrongly) that just because a certain doctrine is a major tenet of faith within the church that everyone in the church knows and understands that teaching. Do not expect people to read your mind.

The vision of the house must be thoroughly and regularly communicated for the good of all concerned. Your vision for the local church will no doubt have a number of facets, each stated succinctly (clear in purpose) in a prioritized list. I always suggest that the vision in its complete form be obviously displayed somewhere in the church house. It can also be permanently printed in your service bulletin, if you use one. Best of all, the vision should be emphasized orally and publicly to all the congregation and on a regular basis. This will keep the same awareness of the vision, just as it does with your regular observance of the Lord's Supper. This presentation should be done by the set man (the daddy best brags on his son). Just emphasize one facet of the vision each week or month; you regularly make announcements, how much more your God-given vision?

Doing this lets everyone get and maintain your vision. The prospect is informed of the purpose of the church, the church family is kept on track by the simple rote of it, and the staff has regular opportunity to constantly measure their effectiveness on the team. *Most* church problems begin with the ignorance or disregard of the vision of the house. No sincere traveler gets bored or upset by the regular checking of his compass.

18. How to Have Proper Staff Relationships

Regularly, a mistake is made in securing staff help initially at the point of need. The set man either waits too long in securing needed help with the vision and becomes discouraged, or he moves prematurely and overloads his budget and/or his strategy by acquiring the wrong person or kind of staff help too early in the ministry.

It is wise and biblical to never acquire staff members until you have fully sought the help of each of the fivefold ministries as their callings are needed within your local church. You do not need a paid or unpaid staff person to do what other fivefold ministers (itinerating within the church body at large) can and should provide at your local church. The apostle should be called in to help with government order, organization, discipline, effective administration, and evaluation of ministry needs. The prophet can help by spiritually stirring up and giving direction to the local church family. The evangelist will fire up and keep fired up the whole church with the opportunity and responsibility of personal witness and the harvest of souls. The teacher with his gift (usually in his particular field) can best communicate an anointed understanding that will not only prompt the congregation to do it, but to keep on doing it.

Why add a staff member to do what God has uniquely provided for through fivefold ministry? Their presence will also help you in realizing what *other* kinds of staff help you really need and the order in which to procure them. If fivefold ministry is not yet resident within your fellowship (which should be the desire of every pastor to see raised up some or all from within his church), seek them out from within your fellowship of local churches.

Choosing a staff member should fill the need for help. Remember: God does not want you wasting time doing things that *you are not* good at. If you are weak in the area of administration, why should you waste money by hiring another pastor? Discern what the specific ministry need is and fill it.

There are basically three sources for acquiring staff help. *One* is to hire a proven minister at large within the church who already has a proven history of accomplishments within his calling. The swap-off for hiring a proven expert is that he comes to you as a virtual stranger to your vision and church family. You have no real way of knowing if he is planning for this move to be but a stepping-stone in his quest for success or if he can adjust to the real DNA of your vision or fellowship.

A *second* source for acquiring a staff member is from a sister church within your fellowship of churches. Although his DNA is quite similar to yours and his character is more easily realized, experience has shown that it is usually difficult to get these people because of petty competition or jealousy that often exists between the churches within the community.

There is a *third* source, by far the best, for acquiring any staff member, and that is to raise him up within your fellowship. He is familiar with your vision, he has acquired your doctrinal understanding, and his character is intimately known. He has a real connection with the leadership and authority of the local church. It is very similar to a son taking his place within the family's business.

The pastor is always sensitive to his spiritual sons and daughters growing up in his church. When the sons or daughters show signs of hunger for more of God or when they publicly express a real interest in getting involved in the service of the Lord, they are encouraged in their pursuit and given opportunities to learn and serve. In a cell church, they will begin to show signs of frustration or boredom at repetitive cell life and desire to be more intently involved, not unlike a pregnant mother trying to play with dolls. It is time to call them aside and have them express their heart's desire, which may well open the door for them to understand where they are and give opportunity for them to take the next step in their calling.

Having dealt with believers for over forty years, with eighteen years of that time spent training the called in our school of ministry, I have found it relatively simple to help the called realize into which of the fivefold ministries they are called. As an apostle, I can spend a day with potentially called people, do a little teaching, and then have them write a brief résumé of their heart's cry to serve God. In reviewing the day and the résumé, I can pretty much discern whether they are called and where they are in the call upon their lives.

When someone is called within the local church, he should be put on a track of preparation within the house until he goes to further his education, receives a call from some other church, or is placed on the staff of the home church. Some churches license someone who is pursuing a calling but has not yet entered his own ministry (office); there is no scriptural precedent for this, but it simply serves like a driver's permit does to student drivers. A called person is normally ordained when he enters into his viable ministry (office).

19. How to Know That Someone Is Right for a Staff Position

There are obvious prerequisites in filling staff positions. We have considered the place of the vision of the house and the sources for seeking out those to serve on the team with us. Let us mention other important areas to consider in screening staff member candidates.

A potential staff member's recommendation should include the soundness of his conversion to Jesus Christ (you cannot take this for granted). It is necessary to know how well he holds to the integrity of the Scriptures in his personal life, the extent of personal holiness in his daily walk, the presence of both the fruit and gifts of the Holy Spirit in his life, his understanding of the call upon his life, his financial stewardship and tithing, a full understanding of his character (both assets and liabilities), and, last but not least, the extent and depth of his private prayer and devotional life.

You should check his secular involvement of life: his past employment, his credit, and his military, criminal, and educational histories, as well as other organizations or groups he has been affiliated with. (I also did a deviate screening for both moral and political involvement before I exposed my people to a potential staff member.) You can well appreciate now the blessing of raising up in-house men and women to be future staff members.

The potential staff member's marriage and family should be screened thoroughly. His health, both physical and mental, should be fully discussed, and his grooming and personal habits realized. His history and attitude concerning divorce and remarriage should be clearly understood. Is his wife a homemaker or a career person, and what will be her visibility within the church? Check to see if he takes regular quality time with his family, and check on his parenting skills. Remember: He will be before your people representing your Christlike values before your congregation and community.

If the proposed staff member is single, he must example your convictions concerning his relationships with members of the opposite sex, both officially and unofficially. Usually a clear understanding is necessary about dating, especially with someone in the congregation, as this has every potential of fostering misunderstandings at best and outright gossip at worst.

20. How to Build Successful Relationships with Your Staff

After a full understanding and agreement on the vision of the house, a staff member must have a clear and comprehensive understanding about the ministry he is to perform. The pastor describes the administrative boundaries of the ministry to be done, while the staff member presents the plan and scope of his strategy for accomplishing his mission. These should be written down, ultimately for the sake of all concerned, now and in the future.

The work schedule must be clearly understood as to the hours per week, days off, holidays, vacations, time off to go out to minister or be ministered to, as well as missions/field trip limitations. All remuneration must be agreed upon up front, clearly defining what the pay will be, both taxable and tax deductible (housing, utilities, insurance, etc.). Make certain that the schedule of pay periods is clearly understood. More anxiety and disappointments develop in this area than can be imagined because of little or no communication. We are servants of God, and money should not have a place to distract our spiritual pursuits and duties; but they can and will. Openness in the financial realm is mandatory.

Another area that must be understood is the role and

responsibility each staff member has when the staff convenes for its regular meetings. The staff member should know the necessity of being present, what reports he is responsible for, and which, if any, are to be in written form.

The pastor is responsible for orchestrating the various personalities of the team and ensuring that the staff meetings and workplace will be harmonious and productive, as some on the staff will have strong, aggressive personalities while others will be quite reserved, leaving the perception of unequal influence within the staff. Each staff member must understand clearly his own area of responsibility and its relationship to the whole vision, as well as the realm of his delegated authority to accomplish his delegated duties. To assist the staff member in this, he needs to have (and continue to develop) a written ministry assignment (job description) to assure that all he does is relevant to the vision of the house.

There is also the matter of *confidentiality.* What part(s) of the staff business is to be held in confidence and to what extent? Some issues are highly sensitive in their nature or timing. One of the most painful issues in pastoral ministry is the leaking of *sensitive* information and then attempting to discover who betrayed the confidence. Staffers need to understand that even if they can *keep* a confidence, others cannot or are insensitive to the nature of the situation (this oftentimes includes their wives or close friends). The rules of confidentiality must be foremost in the mind of all staff members, and even then, specific situations must have additional warnings as to their confidentiality. No one should be offended by these extra precautions.

In the building and maintaining of proper relationships, staff members must have a realistic picture of their places within the staff. A "pecking order" is always present because of natural seniority, program emphasis, or job description. Everyone on staff is important, but position in the vision of the house will cause one or more to have to spend more time with or have a closer relationship with the pastor. Jesus loved all the people; He mentored His twelve, but at times He was more intimate with the three (Peter, James, and John).

The aspect of budget apportionment always requires clarification. The vision of the house should be the determinate factor, not seniority, gifting, etc., of how much money each staff position will be allocated.

The issue of staff *visibility* can present problems unless this matter is clearly stated. By its nature, each area of ministry in the church will vary (high or low) in visibility before the general congregation. This can spawn envy among the staff, and they may need to be reminded that their *audience* is Jesus, while their *ministry* is to their people.

One common misperception often held by staff members concerns their place in the pulpit. There is only one person responsible for filling the pulpit, and that is the senior pastor. He may delegate the pulpit to a staff person on chosen occasions, but the staff person has no place in the pulpit until it is delegated by the pastor. Again, when the itch to preach becomes strong in a staff member, it will help in recognizing the fact that the staff member is coming into his own vision.

It is most important to correctly handle the times of praise and reprimand. Praise should be done as publicly as the situation warrants, and reprimand should be done privately as much as is feasible. Both should be weighed honestly before the Lord and justly given with a sincere heart of love and without any undue postponement. Too little or too much of either one depreciates true service and relationship.

21. How to Discern the Duration of Ministry of Staff Members

One rule of thumb for understanding how long staff members can or will serve on the team is the vision of the house. Many, if not most, staff members are destined to become set men, or senior ministers, with their own God-given visions, and as such they are going to stay on staff only until the time arrives for them to be sent out or set into their own places. I might add that this seems to be a common blind side of many senior pastors. The moment it is recognized that a staff member can no longer stay faithful to the vision of the house, then it is time for him to be sent out with his own ministry. Again, he may be called to serve in another capacity within that house or be called by another ministry to go and serve there. There is no normal time schedule for this to happen, and a pastor may rightfully ask a staff member to commit for a certain time (God's bidding) before he leaves. It is wise to realize this temporal possibility at the start and to always hold in your heart the release of any staff member from the beginning of his service.

It is regrettable, but realistic, to know that sometimes a minister will accept a staff position while having an ulterior motive that this present position will serve only as a stepping-stone to a bigger ministerial opportunity. Proper screening and the discerning of the Holy Spirit at the beginning will hopefully eliminate this problem.

Knowing that a staff member's leaving is almost a certainty, the pastor should be ready to release the staff member and prepare for the leaving to be on the best of terms. To do this, proper preparations and positive announcements should be made to allow his sending out to be a healthy, positive transition that keeps good relationships intact.

On occasion, there will come a time when the leaving of a staff member will be on stressful terms, such as loss of personal integrity, forsaking holiness, or doctrinal error. A clear, clean witness of the local church and pastor *must* be maintained. After all attempts to rectify the problem have failed, then a quick and fair severance is required. You must realize that when a man is having problems internally, he will certainly infect other staff members and the congregation as well. This is virtually impossible to prohibit completely, but handling the matter in a mature and godly fashion will serve to be the best protection from a "wolf" attack. Secrecy is not the essential goal in dismissals, but use discretion in the Holy Spirit to allow the truth to be released so as to protect the relationships within the local church and community. Any severance pay or subsistence will be decided by the depth and nature of the termination.

22. How to Have an Effective Missions Vision in Your Church

It goes without saying that the local church will normally be the refection of the local pastor. Pastors usually have an in-house vision that basically sees the promotion, maintenance, and survival of their local congregations, much the same as a mother's instinct. I have discovered that except for token involvement, the pastoral vision usually limits the local church from its responsibility of Jesus' Great Commission—worldwide evangelization—unless, of course, the pastor has missions engraved on his own ministerial DNA. It will take the vision of the apostle to see the proper *foundational* values of worldwide evangelism to pursue the need and value of a real missions involvement. Again, it will be apostolic vision that prompts church planting and inspires the local church to assume its rightful duty to missions.

Be reminded that it is quite difficult for most local churches to singularly have a major impact on world missions. It is much easier to cooperate with a number of local churches or work with a missions agency to do a significant work.

I always recommend that a church set as an immediate goal to give at least 10 percent of its annual budget to missions work. I consider this a basic minimum, but if you cannot do that, do *something* and get started. Local churches that stay connected to a missions vision will often give upwards to 25 percent and some up to 50 percent of their budgets to the cause of the Great Commission.

It is not always easy to have access to bona fide, productive missionaries, and there are those few who prey as con artists on the generous spirit of the local church. Always have solid recommendations on every missionary or missions project you anticipate giving to. Our fellowship of churches (I.N.L.C.) has its own missions agency that screens, coordinates, and administratively cares for our missionaries. We have our own missionary training school to see that our missions candidates are well prepared. This has saved untold heartaches and disappointments, not only for our local churches, but also for those genuinely called to serve on the mission field to plant churches.

Anything worth doing will require a certain amount of administration and a continual emphasis. There is someone in your congregation who is excited about missions. Let him be responsible to testify, advertise, and keep the fire burning for missions. This will take a goodly amount of encouragement from you as his leader. The immediate and long-term results will be seen within your fellowship. Commitment of service and giving will increase as will a healthy "others' consciousness" (Galatians 5:22, "gentleness"). The local work is important, but not all-inclusive or sufficient, according to Jesus' Great Commission.

23. How to Have an Effective Deliverance Ministry in Your Church

This is an essential ministry now being employed in many churches through the Encounter Retreat weekends. But no matter what form or format you use, deliverance is a viable part of a Christian's growth and the means by which many are able to receive salvation. Unfortunately, because of the negative connotations connected with it, many pastors ignore its rightful place in their Christian ministries.

Please note its place within the ministry of Jesus. In the Gospel according to Mark, seven of the sixteen chapters describe Jesus' deliverance ministry. That is right at half of Mark's Gospel! Seventy-five of the 678 verses report on Jesus' deliverance ministry; that is, 10 percent of His ministry was ministering deliverance.

The one factor that has apparently caused pastors to not get seriously involved with deliverance is the imbalance practiced by a few that gives undue emphasis to demons themselves. It is far more important to *correct* the zealots and carry on with this necessary ministry. To keep a balance here is to place the emphasis of the ministry upon the *people being set free* and not to magnify demons, giving them unjust notoriety.

To have a time officially where new converts can concentrate upon the cross of Christ and see their preeminent need to allow Jesus to assume His rightful place in their lives through the work of the Holy Spirit and trained ministry will facilitate needful deliverance in their lives. The results have been little less than spectacular. New converts leap ahead (years) in their sanctification, making them less susceptible to backsliding and thus *closing* the "back door" of the church. A remarkable 85 percent of your members stay with the Lord and in the church (some denominations have statistics of member retention as low as 21 percent).

The people selected to minister deliverance need thorough training in exorcism and must manifest grace and a deep love to see their brothers and sisters in the Lord free to live their potential. It is essential that the ministry be conducted officially and in a Christ-centered environment.

I mention just a few observations about the ministry of deliverance. Signs of needing deliverance include the following: addictions to <u>anything</u>, torment by mind attacks and emotional instability, defilement of one's person, restlessness, mental illness, unbending religiosity, and seeming inability to repent. To receive deliverance, a person must be willing to receive it. Reasons for people not to receive deliverance include the following: Their repentance is not valid, not being as "wide" as their sins. Real forgiveness of another is lacking. They are staying in the wrong spirit world, or they have no real desire to be set free.

On the other hand, let me share how you can effectively keep your deliverance: Make Jesus *Lord* of all your life, stay in the Word of God, stay in a spiritually healthy environment, attend worship regularly, get and keep your life in divine order, and always wear the armor of God (Ephesians 6:11).

24. How to Revive the Ministry of Healing in Your Church

To have a correct biblical understanding of healing is crucial in establishing and maintaining physical, emotional, and mental healing within your local church. Healing was not a mystical, dispensational work of Jesus while He was on earth, but rather His healing virtue is as viable and extant today as is His forgiveness of sins and His power to cast out demons!

Both Matthew (8:17) and Peter (1 Peter 2:24) affirm Isaiah 53:1–5, ". . . by his stripes we are healed" (this passage in Isaiah is the most widely recognized prophecy of the atonement by every denomination and Christian group). Jesus Himself had no recorded sickness while He ministered on Earth. Pilate assigned the sentence to scourge Jesus first, then ordered Jesus' crucifixion (double jeopardy), thus fulfilling the prophetic words of Isaiah. Jesus took every sin and every sickness and bore them on the cross. He has totally redeemed us from the curse(s) of the Law (Deuteronomy 28:15–68). Healing is in the *atonement.*

Isaiah stated it this way: Jesus was "a man of sorrows" (Hebrew: *pain*) "and acquainted with grief" (Hebrew: *disease*)" (Isaiah 53:3). The only time Jesus was sick in

His earthly life was when He received the stripes ordered by Pilate at His crucifixion, making healing an essential part of His *total* salvation (Greek: *sodzo*).

Healing is not only possible by God's power, but it is an effective part of His (God's) will, as seen by Jesus' answer given to the leper in Matthew 8:3, "I will, be thou clean," and again in Matthew 8:16; 9:6; 10:1; 10:38; 11:5; 12:15; 14:14; and 15:28.

With this as your basic conviction, there is every reason to expect the ministry of healing to take place in your local church, just like you do the ministry of evangelism (conversions). With healing as a basic conviction, you have the faith to expect people to receive their healings. Now you can make this aspect of Jesus' Great Commission an active part of your regular services and daily ministry. So just as you teach and expect every believer to be regularly involved in evangelism (personal soul-winning), so can you likewise expect him to pray for others to be healed, just as Jesus did (John 14:12).

When you extend an invitation in your services for people to be healed, you can anoint them with oil, which is a declaration of consecration, indicating that the candidate for healing has repented of every sin and is hereby ready to receive God's healing virtue. It is important for your people to understand the connection between sin and healing. It is God's will for the believer to deal with present sin in his life and any unforgiveness or offense held against another, so as not to block or hinder the grace of healing.

It is vital for the candidate for healing to understand that improper motivation can hinder his healing. Everyone wants to be free of pain and to be well, but that should not be the principal motivation for receiving healing from the Lord. The chief desire should be for the glory of God; this keeps the heart right.

With proper understanding of the Word and will of God and with true consecration, your people will see healing manifest as a integral part of your ministry daily, as well as in all your church services. It is time for the will of God to be instituted by the church through the complete application of Christ's Gospel without the hindrance of modern religious or cultural notions. It has long been said that "healing is the children's bread"; and the "stripes of Jesus" has long been a realistic way to bring the unconverted to listen and hear the plan of salvation.

25. How to Have a Successful Counseling Ministry in Your Church

The first thing to ascertain is your gifting for this ministry. Many pastors find themselves at odds with pastoral counseling, making excuses such as, "People can get all the help they need from the pulpit." We all realize that that statement is a cop-out. You should counsel to the limit of your gifting, and where that ends, delegate the responsibility to a qualified ministry within your fellowship.

A few simple guidelines help control the continuous and incessant need of some to be counseled. Prioritize your time, and do not deviate except for real emergencies. Most people think you are available for their situation twenty-four hours a day. It has taken them months, sometimes years, to develop their problems, and a solution can usually wait until your next scheduled counseling time. I have found through the years that it is virtually a waste of your time to accept counseling appointments through secondhand referrals. Too often an anxious mother will get you to agree to counsel her wayward son. The trouble is, he will not accept or honor (if he does accept) the appointment, and you are left wasting good time you could well be using for other good things.

Be ready to make referrals when you are dealing with a matter beyond your experience. I would rather look ignorant than to give counsel that is less than the best. Remember that most of the time the counselee, if allowed to talk through his problem, will come to the right conclusion on his own. In any case, you must always tell the truth in love, and most of us can do one or the other well but lack the fortitude to blend both into the counseling session.

The person seeking counsel almost always does not identify the real and basic problem that is causing his trouble. I normally wait until we are in the discussion, and I begin challenging his story when the real problem comes out; then we can get to work on the *right* solution.

If you have not discovered it yet, both parties to the situation must be present to ensure that the most complete story comes forth. When only one person is present for marriage counseling, all you can rightly do is give some good advice.

I have come to learn that it is safer to not counsel another pastor's sheep until you have his blessing to so do. Again, it is wisdom to have the parent's or the guardian's permission to deal with minors. Indeed, it is almost necessary for them to be present for the session.

The age-old counseling trap needs fair warning. The matter of *transference* and *countertransference* must be understood. The average pastor spends a lot of time with members of the opposite sex, especially in counseling, and it is here this trap emerges. If too much time is spent in the sessions or the sessions lose their objectivity, the counselee transfers the solution from the problem-causer to the counselor. Since he is spiritual and clean and intelligent and kind . . . an infatuation takes place. The other side of this scenario is when the counselor succumbs to the counselee's hurts and needs and allows his feelings to get out of hand, resulting in an infatuation. This happens all the time. The seriousness of it is that in that emotional state of involvement, their actions seem justifiably real, and the trap is sprung, with two families and/or the whole church family subjected to the results of this trauma.

As long as we are in the flesh and souls are being won to Jesus, there will always be a viable and necessary place for counseling. People will always need the spiritual guidance and wisdom that God's servants can bring to their lives in restoring godly peace and greater fruition in the kingdom of God.

26. How to Discern Who Needs Counseling and When

Eighty percent of your congregation will fall into two groups: those who feel they will *never* go to a *man* for help and those who have become (usually with our encouragement) counsel *addicts*. A third and smaller group realize the need and value of counsel at critical times in their lives (thank God for these!).

I have found that those who want *you* to make a difference in their situation are codependent and refuse to take responsibility for their own lives; these people can waste a lot of your valuable time that could and should be spent on others who are willing and able to respond correctly to given counsel. The way I do is to give the counselee some homework he has to accomplish by the next session, and if he fails to do his homework or to show sufficient evidence he has tried, I just refuse to go on with the counseling until he gets it done. This always weeds out those who are unwilling to take responsibility for their lives.

On the other hand, you must be ready to discern the factor of demonic control in the counselee's life. He has no power within himself to overcome or even face the reality of his position until he has received deliverance. Uncontrollable sin habits, mental suppression, and fears make counseling useless until his will is back within his control.

Another all too common factor within the ministry of counsel are those who come quickly to receive needful counsel, but, alas, never follow it. The time will come when their problem comes around again, and they usually seek counsel but don't realize why the problem has happened again. They will need to be reminded that their problem is directly related to their procrastination of this matter.

Between the weaknesses of the people who need counsel and the regular pressure you face from the enemy, tempted to "play God" within their lives, you will need fresh grace and serious guidance from the Holy Spirit. Realizing the frailty of all flesh on the one hand and the clear standards contained in the Word of God on the other will produce a holy obligation upon you to close this gap found in all our lives.

27. How to Select Those to Help You with Counseling

As eldership arises in your church, some of them will serve well as counselors within your local church. These men and women know well the vision of the house. They have proven their loyalty to you and have gained the confidence of the congregation through their spirituality and faithfulness. Their commonality with your people makes them open and desirable as confidants. We are all familiar with those in our congregation (and some outside our congregation) who pose as counselors, but whose only desire is to build their own nests of followers and/or control others. These would-be counselors operate with a *controlling* influence, not a Christlike influence.

Be sensitive to the use of professional counselors, for usually these people are expert in personal understanding, but often are insensitive to the whole picture of your Christian environment. A counselor needs more than compassion for those with problems; he needs to hold with a strong conviction the values Jesus has set for our personal spiritual responsibilities.

28. How to Maintain the Highest Counseling Ethics

Many pastors find it difficult to involve themselves in the intimacy of counsel, especially with those of the opposite sex, and maintain a true ethical standard while doing so. Some things to consider: There should be no physical contact. Positioning where and how you and the counselee sit will assist counseling rapport and provide a nonthreatening and nonseductive atmosphere. Better yet, make it a rule in all questionable situations to have a third party present. Let me make a remark here: We all know these basic rules, but time and again, we are tempted to follow the flesh and drift into questionable ethical practices, while all the while the Holy Spirit is warning us of possible trouble.

Never allow the session to be misdirected by personal questions that are basically irrelevant to the problem. It is common sense and good ministry to not allow any counseling ministry to drag on and on. In every immoral scenario I have dealt with pertaining to counseling, the counseling sessions were ongoing by design. Always be sensitive to any buildup or appearance of transference and countertransference.

Some areas of our nation have a higher proneness to

malfeasance of practice for professional services. No one wants to drag his church through such litigation, so your counseling ministry should be conducted with wisdom and the highest of moral standards that exemplify the Lord in every situation, which will minimize any such accusations.

You may be one of those who feel that they have never had any problems or temptations with counseling; you can be sure that any laxness on your part in deviating from impeccable counseling standards will be used by Satan as a well-worn tool to devastate your ministry.

Another potential pitfall of counseling is the pressure it places on your ego. Any semblance of pride opens the door for you as the counselor to become a control freak or seduces you into playing God over the life of the counselee. Your goal as counselor is to lead the person to become responsible and knowledgeable in living his life for Jesus Christ. Codependency upon anyone besides the Lord is a travesty often found in the church. It is your duty to lead every soul you minister to, to be completely free and totally dependent upon the Lord.

One last reminder: Most of us are not knowledgeable in many areas of life that become problems to our people. Only a few of us have any degree of understanding civil or criminal law, medicine, banking and investing, or even in spiritual matters beyond our experience. Of things that we lack understanding, the list is endless. We always want the best help possible for our people. I have always made it a practice to make referrals to competent help for my people when I know little or nothing about a certain area in life. Make a list of and secure permission of experts in every field, and recommend that the counselee avail himself of this help. It would be even more effective if you made an appointment or introduced the person to the expert.

29. How to Maintain Doctrinal Balance in Your Preaching

It never crosses the mind of many pastors that the command of Jesus, "feed My sheep," in John 21:16 includes the *entire* Word of God. Some pastors pay little attention to their responsibility to teach the doctrines of the Bible in a *comprehensive* way. They either take for granted that the major tenets of their persuasion are already understood by their congregation, or they preach only their pet doctrines, just like a person addicted to just one breakfast cereal.

One pastor (really, he is an evangelist) encountered so many people on the streets of his city that in every service he had numerous prospects he had witnessed to just that week. Upon entering his pulpit and seeing them present, he forsook his intended sermon for his church and preached on John 3:16. He was doing this in all three services every week, and before long he had 1,500 people in his church within a two-year period; but he never grew in number beyond that. Those in the congregation won by his evangelism soon began to starve spiritually and left the church, seeking meat for their souls. This is exceptional, of course, but still too many pastors do not feed their sheep with a balanced diet of the Word.

I challenge you to keep a record of each sermon preached and note beside it the doctrine it teaches, and within a year you will see how narrow your spectrum of preaching really is. This will keep you from "hobby topic" preaching.

Most Bible doctrines cannot be adequately taught in just one message (topical preaching). For example, the subject of sin requires at least several messages. Series preaching is not easy for many pastors, but with a little discipline and a lot of study, a three- to six-part sermon series can be formulated. This should be done even before you start preparing the first message. This type of sermon preparation takes discipline, but a plus factor is that the perennial pressure of having to secure a topic for Sunday is already settled. A lengthy series can always be interrupted with a red-hot word from the Lord at any time without adversely affecting the flow of your series then in progress.

Exposition of the books of the Bible is really a favorite of most congregations. I have found during the years of pastoring that our people became Bible literate and doctrinally sound by my preaching verse by verse or chapter by chapter the books of the Bible. In the last pastorate of sixteen years, I preached through fifty-nine books of the Bible, some of them twice. The easy way to do this type of exposition is to read the book numerous times, select the theme (e.g., in the Gospel of John, the idea of "eternal" is in every chapter: eternal God, life, water, Word, etc.), make an outline of each chapter or story-thought in the series before you work on the first sermon, and then build from there. You will be amazed at the timing and oversight the Holy Spirit produces. I cannot mention the number of times where a problem or situation would arise in the church and that week's message addressed *that* problem, obvious to all that it was totally unpremeditated by me—thank you, Jesus!

Most of us do not possess the gift of oratory, and a lot of pastors do not have very much training in homiletics. Furthermore, what they took didn't stick very well. The point is, we can and should seek and not run from any help and constructive criticism that comes our way. Monotone delivery, preaching containing verbal "stuffing" ("ah," "hallelujah," "glory," and "amen"), irritating body language, and lack of genuine eye contact plague many, many preachers. It may be that the lack of responsiveness of our people to our sermonizing is not caused by their lack of spirituality, but by our harsh, ill-prepared, and/or dull preaching.

Prayerfully constructed, anointed delivery can be further enhanced when it contains *visual* content; of course, this requires additional time in preparation. Time is always considered the big enemy to sermon preparation. With overcrowded schedules and multiple daily responsibilities, most pastors fall into the common trap of the devil, which is simply placing higher priority on what is visible and publicly noticed than on what their true functions and callings require.

Prayer and study can become the orphan children of your ministry. To supplement your sinning, most church people relate to their pastors as though preaching good messages was genetically in place, like height. The antidote for busyness is not plagiarizing sermons or trying to operate in giftings you do not possess, but rather it comes from a Holy Spirit conviction that your highest function and responsibility to God and your people is to serve healthy, tasty "meals" *every time* you preach.

Let me identify another "thief" that attends many services: time. Do not waste time in the service with petty nonessentials. There must be sufficient time for the message in each service. To counterbalance that, be certain you plan your timing for the message accurately. Some pastors serve "cold cuts," that is, a nice, brief devotional that is technically called a sermonette, while others preach too long! How do you know you are preaching too long? The less your preparation, the longer your message; you wind up rambling. A sermon is like a business trip, not a sightseeing excursion: it has a definite destination. Again, you can tell if you are preaching too long if you do not stop with your *first* closing; you crescendo your purpose of the sermon to its motivating peak and then start over again building your case. This paralyzes the effectiveness of the message, as well as irritating or confusing the congregation.

A word about repeating your messages: Early in my

ministry, pride had me think that I was less than spiritual if I did not have a newly crafted sermon every time I entered the pulpit. If God has particularly anointed a certain message and the need for that topic comes around again, preach that message again. R.G. Lee of Memphis, Tennessee, preached his message "Payday, Someday" thousands of times with equal effectiveness for many years.

As Jesus stated, your messages are the sustaining, motivating, and challenging spiritual food necessary for your people: "Feed My sheep." Do it with Spirit-guided excellence, both in preparation and delivery.

30. How to Prepare Effective Sermons

Every preacher has his own style for preaching, but the basic rules for sermon preparation remain the same for everyone. Now, there are times when God gives you a message so forceful that you just scratch the verse and the three key words on a napkin while in a restaurant, and as you can expect, it is very effective. However, if you are feeding your church several times a week, you will be faced with the responsibility of ardent and thorough preparation on a regular basis.

You will find that there are three stages in message preparation: the theme or topic, the purpose, and the order. Either the theme or purpose may come first. For example, tithing may be the theme. The purpose is tied to your desired outcome of the message; the need to tithe can be preached, whereas the practice and discipline to tithe is better taught. Know your goal, the purpose of the message, and proceed with your preparation.

As you prioritize your points, order becomes a factor. Often you proceed with A, B, and C, only to stall midpreparation because there is no real flow to the message. Go back and check your order, and the Spirit will give you the best order for your thoughts (or leave one out entirely): perhaps B, A, and C. Oftentimes your emotional bearing is out of sync with the Spirit's logic and order. Speaking of order, many pastors spend more time on the introduction of a message than they do on the closing and application (invitation) of the message (when dressing it is all right to iron your underwear before putting it on, but don't finish your dressing with a wrinkled suit).

When you do comprehensive study and are guided by the Spirit to collect data, make sure you keep your study notes for another occasion. Make some kind of permanent copy of your final draft of the message; failing to conserve the results and product of your study is as foolish as a house builder framing a house all day and just before going home for the day burning it down and starting all over again the next day.

Making room for and following just and constructive criticism is just as essential for your sermon's content as it is for your delivery of it. Have someone you trust evaluate your work, for there is always room for improvement. A "crucifying" approach to critiquing your message is to listen to it on tape. Make sure you have your outline available when you do.

Some preachers feel comfortable using a manuscript; this makes for a polished message (if you read well) but limits the Spirit from interjecting His *present* word. Others use an extensive outline to preach from, while others feel it is imperative to preach without notes. Whichever way, the best rule is to have a permanent copy of your outline, whether you use it in the pulpit or not. It takes an experienced preacher to just start a message impromptu and allow the Holy Spirit to anoint it. For most pastors, if they did start without a planned or prepared message and expected the Holy Spirit to anoint it, it would be like trying to make tea in a boiling kettle without a teabag: all they would have is *hot water.*

Today many are saying that to reach your congregation you must "dumb down" your sermon and put it at, say, an eighth-grade level. Common sense tells you that you are wasting your time preaching over the heads of your people, but at the same time, you must always be stretching their comprehension capability, getting them to a higher level of understanding. I always took the time to enhance their learning by inserting interesting data and by adding to their vocabulary. No one expects an eighth-grader to remain at an eighth-grade level the rest of his life. It is always wise to enforce information by using rote, especially when new data is given.

It never fails, if while preaching I insert a story or an illustration, that the intensity of their attention is greatly magnified. We all know the power of illustrations. There is an unlimited supply of illustration books at the bookstore, but the most powerful stories come from your own experience. If you lack experience, use an apropos story, but know it will be as different as is a frozen TV dinner to a fresh home-cooked meal. Whatever you do, don't make up a story and pass it off as real.

One other word about crafting a good sermon: As imperative as proper study is to your preparation, prayer and the presence of God during the preparation time are *the* factors that will make a good sermon a "God thing." The anointing is as essential during the preparation of a message as it is necessary during the preaching of the sermon.

31. How to Successfully Interpret the Scriptures

Understanding the role the Holy Spirit plays in interpreting the Scriptures is primary. It is He that presented the truth of God (revelation), and it is He that guarded the inscription of God's Word to the human author (inspiration). It is therefore the plan of God that the Holy Spirit brings to us His interpretation of His Word (illumination). The obvious reason so many people, in all their sincerity and expertise, miss the true meaning of a passage of the Bible is at the point of *illumination;* they simply are not relying on or receiving from the Holy Spirit at the time of their interpretation.

There are several rules that will greatly enhance your interpreting the Word of God: (1) The Bible is its own best commentary. Good reference works are a real assistance in Bible study, especially in the area of Bible languages, customs, and history; however, the Scriptures are best and most consistently explained by the Bible itself. I have for years been led to understand one testament by regular reading of the other. Word study (meaning and root study) and character and topic study give depth to Bible understanding.

Your study method will give your Bible study greater meaning and accuracy. Read your passage and *observe* what you are reading. That means the whole passage compared to the details within it. Take note of key terms or phrases. Note also differences as well as similarities (Jesus walking on the water is mentioned in Matthew, Mark, and John, each emphasizing similar facts as well as those not mentioned in the other accounts). The next thing you do is to take the notes from what you have observed and begin to *interpret* them. Ask why, what, when, where, who, and how. Watch that you do not *mis*interpret, *over*interpret, or rationalize your findings. Then you *evaluate* and *apply*. Ask, *Does this finding work for me now? Does it work to God's glory?*

(2) Make certain that your interpretation stays in proper *context,* like one piece of a puzzle having its own unique and qualified part where it perfectly fits.

(3) The principle of the "law of first order," that is, where a subject first appears in the Bible, offers the clearest and purest understanding of that subject or object (e.g., marriage, Genesis 1 and 2).

(4) The revelation of the Bible is *progressive;* the names of God in the Old Testament unfold His person and intent progressively.

(5) The Bible remains consistent with itself. Anytime there is an apparent discrepancy discovered by your study, know that the inconsistency is within your study, not in His Word.

(6) The Scriptures use *symbolic* language (parables, paradoxes, allegories, and types, as well as figurative and literal statements).

(7) Always keep in mind that Jesus Christ is pivotal, the central person and purpose of all Scriptures.

The best way to interpret the Scriptures is through disciplined study. Develop the habit of a consistent time schedule for Bible study (prioritize your life; remember that the study of God's Word is your life's calling). You will discover it helps to have a regular, comfortable, private place that affords easy access to the Spirit and is <u>without</u> interruptions, making sure that all your study tools are present. It is normal for there to be a transition time, going from the natural to the spiritual; it is a good thing to precede your "official" study with your own devotional study. This will cut down on time wasted in trying to become "holy" minded (keep in mind that repentance is essential to every spiritual endeavor).

If you have any aptitude for language study, I recommend the learning of New Testament Greek and Old Testament Hebrew. For those who cannot study biblical languages, always know that there are many good word study helps available.

I say this again, for it bears repeating: Make certain you keep a permanent copy of your serious Bible study notes, as well as of the final drafts of your sermons. Keep a permanent record of all your preaching/teaching as to subject, place, time (mark with a symbol when repeated), and a brief comment on the Lord's blessing upon it.

32. How to Maintain Balance Between Anointing and Authority While Preaching

Many fail to understand the dual empowerment that the Holy Spirit releases when the Word of God is being preached. Paul reminds us in Romans 1:15–16, "I am ready to preach the Gospel . . . it is the power of God unto salvation. . . ." The Holy Spirit graces our preaching with anointing *and* authority.

The *anointing* (the Holy Spirit's enacting presence upon His gifting that He has placed within us; I define it as the unhindered presence of divine activity within us) releases, amplifies, and directs the gifts within a person (personally and/or within the call), whereas *authority* is the presence of God Himself that is resident within His Word and/or delegated to His servants. God's authority is resident in the office (the permanent and official residence of the calling); a person may be called to pastor (fivefold calling), but until he is ordained and set into a local church as the pastor, he has no authority to rule or lead (office).

Anointing will vary as your personal relationship with Jesus varies; authority will change only through delegation by your oversight or as you default in your life (holiness). Again, anointing is in proportion to your gifting (at the same interest rate, $100 gains more profit than does $10); however, the Lord in His sovereignty can increase it according to His will and plan.

Authority is always present within the Word or office to accomplish God's bidding. For example, a pastor may not have as great a preaching anointing (gift) as the visiting evangelist, but in his office as pastor, his messages, perhaps with lesser anointing, will greatly affect the congregation because of his (office) authority as their pastor.

Your goal should be, as you minister, to realize you can operate in both the Lord's authority and anointing, and by maintaining a scriptural relationship with God, both will remain unhindered.

33. How to Acquire Unity Among Believers

Unity is perhaps one of the most misunderstood concepts in the church today. It seemingly defies every attempt to make it happen, leaving most of us with a deep sense of frustration or condemnation. In trying to attain unity as described by Jesus in John 17, believers usually attempt to attain it by starting at the wrong place. To bring people into unity, you do not start first with *doctrine;* Paul states that it first starts with the Spirit (Ephesians 4:3 and 13).

It is quite obvious it is nigh impossible to get anyone to agree with you completely on doctrine, and even if the person does, it won't be for very long. Unity is only achieved in stages (like going up stairs). Unity starts with *a* commonly held truth, and then unity grows as we agree, truth by truth. This way unity, like marriage, remains intact even when something else causes a disagreement. True unity is not shattered in the presence of disagreement, but only by the absence of truth.

Unity, like a chain, is forged by truths linked together in love. The presence of disagreement (usually based on wrong communication) does not nullify unity anymore than if you went to the store to buy an article only to discover you lacked a few cents of the purchase price. You would not throw away the money you already had; no, you would go and get the money you lacked and return to buy the object. Let us act in the same wisdom towards unity. The bottom line is this: Start with a truth and walk in that unity while seeking for more truths on which to agree.

Another factor about unity is that it is only viable when there is a *relationship* (not a contract or creed) in place. Relationships are made like a patchwork quilt, many and varied pieces sewed together in a recognizable pattern. Realize, of course, that relationships, by their very nature, are damaged by pride and selfishness (both of which are "scissor blades" to the fabric of unity).

Again, unity is quick to recognize and embrace every similarity while at the same time not allowing differences to divide. It's just like the way you enjoy your children when they mind you but do not disown them when they don't, because you are still *one* family. Remember: Rejoice in the unity you have, like a savings that grows only as you work and add to it, affording you with security and peace.

34. How to Cope with the Parachurch, Civic Affairs, and Secular Involvement

The parachurch is a modern entity that is predicated upon several fallacies. The first is the lack of understanding of the fivefold callings of God. Many believers want to serve God in areas that their church is not involved in, either by neglect or that area not being a part of the local vision, so they go outside the church to "minister." And because they believe that what they are doing is essential and "Christian," they feel the church at large should accept what they are doing as "church." They may well be right; for example, Youth With A Mission does a superb job with evangelism, but it is not a church. Parachurch groups do not have the DNA of a New Testament church because they are self-limited to usually just one aspect of what the New Testament defines as church (life). Ministry (and mostly just a phase of ministry) does not constitute being a church. The church is responsible for order, government, discipleship, discipline, ordinances, fellowship, and relationships. Limiting one's activities (no matter how biblical they are) to operate without the fullness of a New Testament church is to practice confusion and opens the door to disunity in the body of Christ.

The second reason for the existence of parachurch ministries is the obvious forsaking of certain Christian responsibilities by the church, such as an effective pro-life (anti-abortion) ministry, caring for the poor and hungry, and many other areas of neglect. The best alternative to getting the church to fulfill its responsibilities is not to separate and form an *extralocal* entity, but to pray and see these needful areas of ministry reclaimed by the local church; to do so, you might have to relocate your affiliation to a local church that contains your passion within its local vision.

Thirdly is the confusion about separation of church and state; the Constitution is very clear about Congress not making any law to limit the free exercise of religion, but it does not say one word about the church's influence or involvement upon the affairs of the state. The Bible fully declares the responsibility of every Christian to influence his community, society, and the world with the truths and ways of God. The church has every right and responsibility to preach and influence the affairs of men in every realm of life. Just because something is called "secular" does not remove it or those involved in it from the jurisdiction of righteousness. It is the church's responsibility to be involved in the affairs of men and not relegate it to parachurch ministries. Nowhere in the New Testament is there found a place for Christian ministry and life outside the local church. This is why there are always multiple expressions within a community of local churches, each with a varied but complementary vision and giving wholeness to the purposes of God.

Not every local church has a vision that is limited by the set man of that church. When you align yourself with the place God would have you serve, be certain that vision encompasses your heart's conviction of ministry. As a pastor, you should make clear to each new member what the vision of the house is; this will preclude a lot of misunderstanding down the road. There is not much room for or need of a Navy torpedo man on an Air Force reconnaissance aircraft, but both skills are necessary and have their place in winning a war.

35. Five Characteristics of a True Pastor

There are three kinds of men found filling the office of the pastor today. One is the man who knows he is called, but every sign and teaching of the New Testament indicates clearly that his calling is *not* pastoral. He does not have a burden for the sheep, or he has no skills (gifting) that evidence a pastoral calling. He understands his sheep like most men have figured out their wives: not much at all! One major sign that he is not pastoral is his "self" passion for ministry (e.g., radio or TV) or his ability to operate programs within the church. He administrates the affairs of the church well but has little to no relationship with his flock. His pulpit is the place where he expands his ministry rather than building up his people. Find out and know what your calling is before you claim to be or try to be a pastor.

A second kind of man has a real pastoral interest in his flock but has yet to move in the authority of his office as pastor. He has a good flock, but he can't get them to the "next pasture," having no clear and well-communicated vision. He usually demonstrates little ability to delegating responsibility, so he spends a great deal of time doing what he is not good at. He is prone to keep himself isolated, resulting in little or no accountability, which inevitably shows up in his sheep. Area cultural values, expectations of others, or denominational limits smother any drive he may have, leaving his church to look like an algae-covered pond when it could be a white-water rapids river inspired by the Holy Spirit.

The third example of a pastor is one who definitely has a shepherd's heart. He loves people and covets his sheep. He radiates the Father's love and protection. He shines with the grace of a mother's desire to provide and just enjoys the family of God in a local setting. He really desires to disciple everyone who comes under his covering.

Let me share with you five (of many) signs of a true pastor. *First,* if you are a true pastor, you *lead* your people into true worship (relationship) with the Godhead. Your people come to church to minister to God more than to be ministered to. The pastor and the worship team are in true harmony, releasing peace upon the whole scenario. Each service is a time for building relationships vertically and horizontally in the presence of God.

Second, your people feel *safe* in God's house and under your ministry as you release the flow of spiritual authority without abusing them. The sheep are encouraged (without condemnation) to be free to do their best for the Lord, as well as to spiritually express themselves without feeling coerced.

Third, your people feel *"pastured"* because they are! How many of the people attending your services just attend your church but are not involved with your vision? They come because they like the preaching, music, or some program you sponsor. There is a certain commitment and bonding that takes place before you become someone's pastor; this usually happens when the person faces a crisis (a birth, a death, or a trauma) in his life, and he calls on you and receives your help.

Fourth, your people have a real sense of *ownership.* This is *their* church. Jesus invited them. The Holy Spirit has accepted them, and they see the *Father* in the man of God, that is, you. They have discovered what their place is in the church. They appreciate being discipled and used in God's service and becoming a real part of the vision of the house.

Fifth, your people realize their places in being a part of something bigger than they are and have a viable part of the Great Commission in *giving, going* (short-term missions trips), and being used in their giftings.

36. What Is Spiritual Authority?

We all know and appreciate the fact that God is the author and owner of all things, including every principle of life and truth. Just as there is only one law (kind) of gravity, so it is with *authority.* All authority belongs to God (Romans 13:1). When authority is present, it is always *delegated,* whether in the civil, religious, physical, or spiritual realm. The source of all authority is God. One principle of His authority is that it *flows* in only one direction: *downward,* without exception (just like gravity).

The problem in many churches (their government) is that there is usually an attempt to contradict God's law of authority. For example, all too often, there is a group (board) within a local church that thinks it is their duty to watch over the pastor (designates salary, term of office, vision of the house, and many other factors that should be determined by the set man). This is an unauthorized (illegal) use of authority by attempting to have authority flow *upward* (try that with gravity!).

Seriously, the Roman Catholic Church has the closest form of New Testament government (excepting the error of an [infallible] pope). This prompts us to see and accept what the apostle Paul did in having each local pastor set in, ordained, mentored, and made *accountable* to the apostolic/prophetic ministry team that functioned from outside that local church (extralocal). The International Network of Local Churches utilizes the same plan of accountability to spiritual authority. Each pastor has a presbytery of three apostolic men (extralocal) to whom he is accountable. This keeps spiritual authority in the correct and downward flow.

Authority is really the *right* (divinely delegated) to make decisions and act upon those decisions. Authority provides for *stability,* that which gives confidence and direction all at the same time. Authority provides for *protection* from self-indulgence as well as from the enemy's wiles. Again, authority provides for *security,* an umbrella of shelter that is both durable and real. At the same time, authority quells subversion, confusion, and condemnation.

The context (balance) of divine authority is the consistent, conscientious practice of *serving,* as so clearly demonstrated by the life of Jesus. As a true leader, the more authority one is responsible for, the quicker he is to become a servant to all.

All deviation from true authority is rebellion against God, its ultimate source. Should a *delegate* of spiritual authority waver from the truth, it is better for the *followers* to allow God to deal with the leader. Rarely is one ever blameworthy for submission to wrongly implemented authority; furthermore, God always has the means to deal with wayward leaders. The classic rule as demonstrated by Peter in Acts 4 of refusing to obey wrongly applied authority is based solely upon the fact that God's known will obviously contradicts His human delegate. Then noncompliance (disobedience) is always with an attitude of true submission, courtesy, and humility.

True authority is graced with the presence of anointed wisdom, clarity of vision, and passion for righteousness, as well as obvious giftings. Even when there are apparent personality differences or even conflicts, this anointing, as a beacon, lights the way of God's will.

There accompanies delegated authority a certain loneliness (averting familiarity and misjudgment) that is not to be confused with aloofness, or exclusiveness, which is pride-centered. This is why it is necessary for peer relationships to be extant, as well as to have ongoing "father mentoring." These are so obviously necessary.

You need not and should not seek authority. It is always granted by God (or His delegate) in the right amount and exactly at the right time. On the other hand, it is normal and healthy to seek opportunity to practice your giftings. Authority is absolutely essential to every calling but should never be taken for granted; it is quite similar to a law officer who wears a pistol. He is constantly conscious of his weapon, as to how and when to use it and its power to do good or evil. Authority is a "God thing," just like life; the more we are conscious of His presence, the better stewards we are of it.

37. What Is Church Discipline and How Does It Work?

Jesus taught in Matthew 18:15 the principle of forgiveness as practiced within (His body) every local *church.* The true believer, whether he has been sinned against or has sinned *(trespassed)* against another body member, should immediately, upon this being revealed to him, seek out that brother(s) and grant or request forgiveness (whichever the case may be). This, said Jesus, must be done immediately and *privately* to restore and maintain true fellowship in that local church.

Jesus went on further and said if that person(s) does not accept or acknowledge your openness to restore peace, then you approach him a second time, taking with you two other believers who are mature and unbiased, and make your appeal again. If the brother accepts your plea, you have gained peace within the fellowship. If this person does not accept or grant forgiveness as arbitrated by the two people, then, said Jesus, the matter must be brought to the local church *(body)* publicly in a formal (called) meeting where the officers of the church preside and deal with this matter. Again, the act of repentance will restore the brother back into fellowship and will affect the whole body, which (from years of experience in practicing this, I have numerous and exciting testimonies) opens the door to the spirit of revival within the local church. If the guilty person does not repent and seek restoration, Jesus went on to say, then the local body must relate to the unrestored brother as to a *heathen* (a lost, unregenerate person), in love and witness to him. This will clarify his spiritual condition to him and to the community.

This teaching of Jesus' fully illuminates each believer's responsibility to keep every relationship in a state of holiness, both outwardly and inwardly. Subliminal offenses among believers are the greatest *cancer* to Christian relationships and are stopping revival from taking place in almost every local church.

When I teach on this subject, the question always arises whether you always have to do the third step in front of the whole church. My answer to this is as follows: The breadth of light to be shone on the restoration attempt is always equal to the notoriety and nature of the sin involved. Definitely, a leader or a person in office or the public eye must be dealt with before the congregation to uphold the standard of righteousness before all. I personally have always done step three before the whole assembly in a prominent service and have always, without exception, had positive results, with a revival spirit taking hold of the church. A few brief testimonies may help bring affirmation to my practice.

We had a couple that decided to live together, despite their clear understanding and affirmation of their wrong decision. She was a separated wife, but not yet divorced, and was teaching a class. He was a new member in the body and still controlled by a maverick, macho spirit. He was unemployed. They came in for counsel (to seek permission from me to allow them to perpetrate this sin). For an hour, I debated with them about this step towards hell, to no avail. I then warned them that I would ask them publicly to recant or leave the fellowship. The very next service, I had to announce their demise and their choice to leave the fellowship. The service was laced with visitors, and I felt squeamish, being sensitive to their presence; but I went ahead as protocol demanded. After the service, several of the visitors sought me out and were thoroughly blessed by the operation of church discipline, which they had heard about but had never witnessed in all their Christian lives.

Another time an adult son (saved member) of one of our church leaders and sheriff of the county where the church was located was caught running moonshine. Even though he was raised as a believer and married, in a moment of excitement he accepted a challenge to deliver homemade whiskey across the state line. He was promptly caught by the state police, jailed, and bonded on a Saturday morning. The community was relatively small, and news traveled rapidly; I, along with the rest of the town, knew about this in a matter of a couple of hours. I immediately proceeded to his home, and when he came to the door, he fell into my arms with apparent grief. I invited him outside, and we knelt down by his truck and settled the issue with the Lord vocally.

We went back into the house, and he repented to his wife; then we stepped next door where he did the same to his parents. Then I told him that he was to come before the church tomorrow, Sunday morning, and share his repentance to the church, his spiritual home. He agreed. Sunday morning he came—late. Church went on as usual, except for the craning necks and gawking eyes. At the end of the service, I had him come down to face, with me, the congregation. He reported his repentance to God and asked their forgiveness. As usual in these situations, I told the congregation to come down and hug and receive his lovely wife and him back into true fellowship. They did. Revival broke out for several months.

The story continues. The young man was brought to court for breaking the law, and his father asked me what they should do because the rest of the seven men involved were going to plead innocent. I reminded them that he had publicly confessed and dealt with the sin, and to plead innocent now would be to belie his stand before God and his church. He agreed to plead guilty. I wrote to the judge, who was a believer, and explained what had happened with the young man and his repentance before God and the church. The judge released him without charge, and the other six men were found guilty and served six months in jail. Praise Jesus! This is the power of church discipline.

Church discipline has proven to be a dynamic factor in the life of a local church, without exception, clearing the spiritual air and releasing a spirit of unity, brotherhood, and love that spawns a spirit of revival. Remember that as Moses closed out the book of Deuteronomy, on numerous occasions he called for the execution of deliberate offenders for the sole reason to keep Israel strong and in the presence and will of God. When you deal with the cancer of sin within the body of Christ swiftly and thoroughly in the manner stated by Jesus, you will be able to keep your people on the cutting edge of God's purpose for His church.

38. What Does the New Testament Teach About Church Government?

As a pastor, your vision, purpose of your calling, and responsibility as pastor of your local church is to *build* the house as you *shepherd* your flock. This vision is primarily vertical in nature. There is another vision that precedes and coincides with your vertical vision and is necessary for the establishment of a local church, and that is the placement of a proper *foundation.* This vision is horizontal in scope and usually falls within the calling of the apostle.

One of the initial things a pastor needs to do is to connect with apostolic ministry and plan a proper foundation for the new work or review with an apostle the foundation of his existing church, as to its "wholeness." (I have developed a "Church Profile" that is instrumental in accomplishing this essential task; write to I.N.L.C., P.O. Box 217, Gonzales, LA 70707-0217). One of five major areas that must be correct in order to have a good foundation for your church is the type of *government* that will be (or should be) in place. Within the whole of the Bible, there is only one form of government that is practiced successfully, and that form is a *theocracy.*

A theocratic government is where God (Father, Son,

and Spirit) is the source of authority and proprietor of the vision. In both testaments, this is the only form of government that appears, despite the fact that in church history there have been several other types of government attempted. History records that these illicit forms of government cause churches to stagnate in mission and stagger into ineffectiveness. One of these types of government is the *episcopal* (bishop-run) government, such as the Roman Catholic Church. The Reformation produced a second form of church government, known as *presbyterian* (council-run) government, which allows for a bureaucracy to rise and cause the erosion of mission and loss of effectiveness. A third type of church government found today is the *democratic* (people-run) government, which has caused the "priesthood of the believer" to usurp the sovereignty of God and His will.

In the book of Acts, we find a *theocratic* government where the Holy Spirit (God) governs the church. It is He who has inscribed the clear pattern for church government. The New Testament states that Jesus gave (called) fivefold ministry to plant, oversee, and disciple the church(es). Clearly, in the New Testament, there was no viable church functioning without the presence of ministry, and usually it was an interworking team of fivefold ministry. The apostle was *sent* by divine commission to start local churches. The prophet *lighted* the way, keeping divine presence upon the vision. Evangelists *fueled* the vision of the local church through their winning souls in the local area. In due season, pastors (shepherds who were either called out of the local body or sent in to see the local church flourish and multiply) arose. These men, having the vision of the house, were set in by the apostles and prophets. Teachers were called in to *refuel* the vision with additional truth.

As stated above, God's authority for governing flows downward. In the New Testament, we never see anyone in the local congregation outside of ministry ruling or overseeing a local church. Despite the American democratic culture, the New Testament church is never depicted as having any form of democracy, councils, sessions, or schools of cardinals within its framework of church government. The New Testament church today should be *theocratic,* governed by the Holy Spirit, who uses fivefold ministry to orchestrate His work.

A word about elders: This generic term is used to describe those who function in delegated authority within the local church. Even the pastor or a residing apostle serves as an elder. This present group of elders assists the set man (pastor) in governing the flock. They do not *govern* the set man; the set man is accountable to the apostolic oversight (extralocal) that has been in place (or should be) since the foundation of the church. Remember the law pertaining to spiritual authority: Spiritual authority only flows down from God, without exception.

39. What Is an Apostolic Presbytery?

Answers to many of the questions asked concerning the concept and application of spiritual covering for a local church can be found in the understanding of apostolic presbytery. The book of Acts, Chapter 13 and following, tells us that Paul was sent out from the church at Antioch (apostolically) and by the Holy Spirit to plant new churches. His God-guided procedure was to ascertain the location (city), find or make converts, and then set up a local (home) church. Paul then assumed his apostolic responsibility to visit regularly; offer correction where and when needed; and to discern, disciple, and set in fivefold ministry in each local church. This is the New Testament procedure, and it demonstrates to us how to have each church covered with apostolic (team) oversight.

Mimicking the example set forth in Acts, I.N.L.C. (along with many other duties) has an apostolic team to provide a three-man apostolic team to assist, to relate to, and to grant oversight to each local church. We consider the apostolic team as an extralocal entity for the purpose of covering. Extralocal clarifies the fact that the local church is the building block God uses to carry out the Great Commission successfully. The local church set man (he may be a pastor in calling or one of the other fivefold ministries) is responsible for the vision of the house (the building and expansion of the local church). Each local church runs its own affairs within that vision.

The set man of the local church is personally accountable to the three-man apostolic presbytery, and the two entities maintain a close, viable relationship through mentoring. The only time the apostolic presbytery comes into the local church is by invitation of the pastor or should others in the ministry (elders) need their help. The lead presbyter (usually the ministerial father to the pastor) has the pulpit at least once a year to foster a healthy relationship with the congregation.

The apostolic presbytery can be called in when a leadership problem comes to an impasse: the set man defaults in doctrine, morals, or ethics, or should the pastor die or be killed. They assist the local work to carry on its vision and responsibilities until an interim pastor is recognized. The apostolic presbytery will set in the new pastor.

This relationship between the apostolic team and the local church affords diligent, genuine covering while at the same time precluding the obvious pitfalls of the other two extremes: denominationalism and independent churches. Every denomination affords covering, government, and oversight that usually are too radical or too removed from the local church. The denomination usually possesses the vision and spoon-feeds it to the local church; this builds frustration within the pastor, who is really the vision carrier of the work. On the other hand, independent churches run an even higher risk of missing their potential in Christ. Independent ministries have a tendency to become isolated, self-centered, and suspicious (of other churches). Without true accountability, they have no way of recovering from doctrinal error or immorality within the ministry.

Many ministers confuse responsibility with accountability. Responsibility is to your people and involves your work. True accountability is to a person (above you in spiritual maturity and office) and involves your character. You must have both to be a true servant of the Lord.

40. Who Controls the Vision?

In Number 14 we identified vision: "*Vision* is the awareness of God's *purpose* for your life ministry. God is a God of purpose (reason, cause, plan, and strategy)." Can vision be delegated? Who owns the vision? Who decides that the vision is valid? These are governmental questions.

Vision is for a ministry, but it comes through a person whom God calls and qualifies to see that vision take place. The apostolic vision is horizontal (foundational and world-reaching). The local church vision is vertical ("house" building and evangelical). In a local church, one vision is built upon the other. Each ministry will be working together and complementing the whole.

Vision cannot be delegated anymore than you can delegate your life. The vision outworking or strategy will always be shared and can be delegated. Sometimes a minister has too much ambition, which is called vision; he assumes by ego or ignorance to accomplish too much or too varied a goal that he has neither giftings nor calling to do. On the other hand, some men have little or no vision; they, through laziness or lack of relationship with the Holy Spirit, assume that the Great Commission is their personal vision. This is not their vision, but the mandate for the whole body of Christ before the end of time. Other pastors think that facing each day with its numerous demands upon their time is vision enough; this lack of direct inspiration and pointed purpose allows for stagnation within the local church. Sometimes a good vision is present but is poorly communicated, leaving the congregation aimless and lethargic.

It is always the privilege of the apostle (presbyter) to assist the local pastor in managing his vision of the house. I have spent countless hours identifying, defining, strategizing, and administrating the vision (or lack of it) with local church pastors. There is nothing more exhilarating than possessing and processing the vision God has given you for your life. As an apostle, it is my privilege to walk with pastors and assist them with their visions. As I tell pastors (and have for many years), "My vision is to see *your* vision excel."

41. How Influence Complements Spiritual Authority

God in His sovereignty places in balance everything He has created. Since His authority rests so much in the hands of leadership, God grants *influence* to those whose place it is to follow (being under authority). Influence is the balance to authority in several ways: It helps keep in check the abuse (excesses of the flesh) of authority. It affords the gifting and wisdom of each one under authority to complement the purpose and vision of God. It recognizes the unique place and rights of every individual in the group (church).

As with all things from God, influence is based upon our faithfulness to Him and in being good stewards of our lives. The best illustration of *influence* is seen in the context of marriage. The Lord has delegated the husband as the head of the home, while at the same time He makes available (tremendous) influence to the wife in the relationship. I can report that I am in authority over my home (God's delegated authority), and at the same time, my wife exercises tremendous influence over every aspect of our home.

The perfect example of someone exercising influence is shown by the life of Queen Esther. In a time of desperate danger, she was instructed by the counsel of her uncle,

Mordecai, to use her (great) influence to intervene on behalf of all. So along with the prayer and fasting of the people of God, she came to use her influence (the greatest thing she had) with the king. Through her influence, she protected not only her own life, but also the lives of all her people, stopping the annihilation of her race and bringing them into a place of honor before the king.

So it is for all members of the local church; they can, by the grace and purpose of God, establish the *influence* they have before the congregation of God. Every person can become an influencer, just like Jethro was to Moses or Daniel was to Darius or Aquila and Priscilla were to Apollos. But they need to be taught to realize its presence and to cultivate their portion of influence granted by God to them.

42. How to Be Sensitive to the Holy Spirit in Every Service

Experience has shown me that no less than 65 percent of pastors suffer in this area, and most do not even realize they do. They lack what I would term "service sensitivity." Let me ask you: Do you find yourself hesitant to change the order of a service? Do you feel you are possibly interrupting the Holy Spirit's flow to stop someone who is ministering? Do you have the feeling after a service that you missed it somewhere? Are you plagued with doubts about interrupting a service when you feel it should be flowing in a different direction? I want to implant in you the parameters of authority that allow you to follow the Holy Spirit's timing that is essential for *every* service and to show you how to activate your assertiveness, allowing Him full access in every service.

You must ever be aware of the fact that as moderator of each service, you are the key (human side) to the Holy Spirit's orchestration of success during the service time. You are to be *in charge* as the Spirit *leads* you and as you *guide* the people, just as a conductor follows the musical score and guides the orchestra. You have no right to defer to someone who will usurp the time and lead the service astray. You are not going to have some mystical sign prompting you to change direction or implement a planned or unplanned aspect of ministry (silence included; silence does not mean someone missed his cue).

As all persons involved have assignments to accomplish, you must see that they obediently carry out their parts in a timely and anointed fashion. They cannot deviate without your coordination. No one should take it upon himself to preach along with his assignment to give announcements. If a singer is to bring forth a solo, he has no authority to self-appoint himself to sing two or three more songs. Testimonials should either be agreed upon or stay within the time frame and topical flow of that service. Anyone on the rostrum or anyone who comes before the people must realize that *he* is not *the* program. Do not allow a service to drift off onto some "rabbit trail"; this is irreverently interrupting the Holy Spirit. Remember: You are directing the traffic for the Holy Spirit; He is going to talk to you, guide you, and notify you of any change of program. You would not stand for someone to interrupt your sermon; do not let someone interrupt the Holy Spirit at any time in the service.

The people will come to realize that you are not a dictator, but rather that you are following the Holy Spirit; they will soon become grateful for your sensitivity and your authority being present. Remember that you do not owe anyone anything. You are responsible to discern the motivation of all those scheduled or attempting to be on the program. The same authority that works through you, allowing them to minister during that service, also keeps them from drifting into carnal pursuits. The Holy Spirit does not run a three-ring circus, nor is He putting on a talent show, much less a "Christian book and gift shop" or a "classified ad" service.

When notified by the Spirit, do not hesitate; God always brings immediate confirmation to the situation and what *you* are expected to do about it. Have confidence in your call and your role as moderator. The Spirit of God will lead you in graceful and meaningful transitions during the service; do not portray signs of indecision and lack of assurance. Remember, too, that you will have to deal with people's feelings, but meditate on that after the service, not while it is going on. You are responsible to the Holy Spirit for the pulpit and each service.

Once while serving as an associate, I was given charge of a midweek service while the pastor was away. Our services were very lively and appeared to be spontaneous, but the Holy Spirit always led and guided each time. Being a novice and not sure of my delegated authority, as well as being self-conscious about my responsibility, I did not stay close to the presence of the Spirit. Normally before prayer we received testimonies to accentuate the power of our praying. A sweet lady member in our church, who usually brought a guest (amen!), had with her a huge, formidable-looking woman(?) The Spirit of God tried to warn me, but as I said, I was preoccupied with the message I was to bring and ignored the prompting. This guest asked to testify. When I gave her permission, she promptly stood up and turned her back to me to face the congregation. Ten seconds into her report she, with no reason, began to attack The Gideons International. At the back of the auditorium, one of our faithful ushers was busy, but when he heard her attack, being a loyal Gideon member, he lashed out at her. Their argument got louder and louder. I had lost the service! In desperation I *shouted* at the top of my lungs, "Shut up!" Quiet descended upon the service, but no peace. Then a meek little college kid whined where all could hear, "I don't feel the love of God here." That finished the grieving of the Holy Spirit. I tried congregational singing—a waste of time—and went into my message, which I had no strength to finish. I dismissed the service early and spent the night in prayer. A hard lesson was learned that night.

43. How to Deal with Offenses

Offenses are probably the largest sector of sin within the church; therefore, a pastor must be highly sensitive to and discerning in the matter of offenses. He must first maintain that forgiveness is the *only* successful remedy for offenses. Secondly, he must understand that most offenses are kept subliminal, buried deep within the soul, causing gaping, unhealed wounds in the soul that, within the church, are usually covered with mock courtesy and religious reasoning.

A simple example of this (you know many incidents within your ministry) follows: Mrs. J—— came forward *again* (about the fourth time in three weeks) during the Sunday morning invitation time to be prayed over for a specific healing. As usual, I began to anoint her with oil and to pray for her (again, the fourth time) when the Spirit of God abruptly stopped me and gave me a word of knowledge concerning her: "She has a deep-rooted unforgiveness (an offense) toward her husband, and I cannot heal her while that remains!" I lowered my hand and asked her to open her eyes and look at me. I asked her if she had any unforgiveness towards anyone. She looked straight at me and replied that she had no unforgiveness presently toward anyone. I then told her the word the

Holy Spirit had just given me about her offense towards her husband. Her face clouded up as she reported that she had tried to forgive him, but he was not saved and did not love God and had not changed. I explained to her that she had an offense toward her husband and she must set it down by forgiving him now, once and for all. She said she could not at that time. She never did. He died, and she still has that same physical problem to this very day. This kind of self-centered rationale, embossed with religious or pious ideas, is rampant in our churches today.

It is also necessary to realize the difference between being brought under conviction and being offended. Conviction is based upon the truth and deals with the principle found in God's Word of "right" and "wrong"; many evade conviction of their sin by saying they are offended. This is really not the case; they are under conviction. If they do not repent, they just may soon have an offense against God.

Being offended is a matter of one's will; it is a personal choice, taking personally what someone said or did and willfully making it an *offense.* When one becomes offended, it is always, without exception, about, over, or centered upon a *person;* it is personal. Someone can become *embarrassed* over a situation or become *hurt* by an opinion. I can become *offended* through a situation, but it becomes an *offense* when I personally blame you. I might forgive the action but hold you personally to blame for the situation. In time I can even forget the act or scenario, but I do not release, or forgive, you, the one who supposedly perpetrated the act. This is an *offense*.

In 2 Corinthians 6:5; 10–11, we are reminded that we are not to become offended when we are misunderstood or falsely accused (v. 5), cause someone to be offended by what we do (v. 10), or cause someone to become offended by what we are or what we have (v. 11). Our nature is to *harbor* the offense and not forgive it immediately. These "time-honored" offenses are usually kept low-key or private, and they are often covered with a kind of religious reasoning (no unforgiveness is sanctioned by the Gospel) and thus become the very wall that blocks God's promises and blessings from flowing in our lives, thereby hindering our service to God and hocking the anointing upon ministry.

44. The Place and Purpose of Restoration

Too often today, the biblical process of restoration has been reduced to or limited to repentance. They are not the same. Of course, repentance is initial and essential to restoration, but we cannot stop there

Restoration is founded upon true repentance. True repentance stands (like a table) upon four legs: admission of sin, seeing the sin from the viewpoint of God, turning (life change) from that sin, and making every attempt at restitution for that sin. There must be personal identification with the thought or ungodly act. This is coupled with the conviction that the sin in the eyes of God is heinous and damning. Then there is a historical sorrow and turning back from that sin (repentance), and finally every attempt is made by the sinner to repay or replace the result of that sin. For example, if I steal an item, I replace that item or attempt to do so.

If I take a finely finished wooden chair and dump green paint on it, it is for the most part no good as it remains. Repentance is taking sandpaper and paint remover to bring the chair back to the bare wood; there is no way to remove the paint without damaging the original finish. Restoration is the bringing back of the original finish, which takes time and skill. If done properly, no one will ever know the chair was damaged in the first place; this is restoration.

When ministry (or any leader or person) falls, like the lost coin of the woman in Luke 15, we must not stop caring and reaching out until he is found. Of course, this depends initially upon his willingness to repent and accept restoration.

In I.N.L.C., when a minister falls, we seek him out, ascertain and judge the case, immediately set him down and out of his present place of responsibility, and set him into a program of restoration, which is usually at another place for recovery. The man's call is not erased by sin; it is rendered officially ineffective by sin.

One must apply wisdom in the process of restoration. The publicity, duration, and the place and kind of restoration must be directly related to the station of leadership and the duration and depth of the sin committed. The more *public* the person's ministry was, the more public the restoration must be. The more influential his ministry was, the more *time* it will take to restore his credibility. There is a huge difference between a national leader and an elder both falling into adulterous relationships. The same standard for repentance is upon both, but the process of restoration is different.

In a certain state a while back, I came to a church just in time for the first service of a planned meeting of several days. The music was lively, and the people really followed the minister of music enthusiastically. However, I was not comfortable with the overall spirit of the service. Having to get right into the pulpit, I put off my notions. They started up again as we went to the pastor's home for refreshments after the service. Finally, I just told the pastor my leading, that something was wrong in the life of the minister of music. The pastor just bragged on the man's enthusiasm and way with the people as he led worship and the fact that he had been with them for several years now. I prayed that night with no relief of my concern about the matter.

In the morning, I asked the pastor to let us speak with the minister of music. The minute I began chatting with the man, the Spirit of the Lord came over him, and he began to sob unrelentingly. In minutes he was confessing his affair with two of the more prominent women in the church. He repented, and we first faced the ladies for verification and then the man's wife and three teenaged daughters. His family was grimly hurt.

The pastor wanted to release the man, but I persuaded him to see him fully restored. The man repented to the church and was then sent to a church in another state to start as just a regular church member and work his way back into his ministry, which took two years. Now the man is serving God more effectively than ever before, with a healed and loving family at his side. This is the power and effectiveness of restoration.

There is a tendency to bypass the making of the repentance public. Again, the person's place in leadership should decide how public the repentance should be. If a man falls into sin and confesses this to his wife and pastor and the man and wife make up, the repentance and restoration should be quiet. If, however, an elder or leader in the church is guilty of an affair, the repentance should be to all the people he has affected. Time and again, I have seen this bring revival to the local church.

Again, rarely is a fallen pastor able to be immediately restored to or within his present church; he has lost too much credibility and will damage the mission of the local church. Churches bonded together can work together to assist fallen ministry to be restored and set back into fruitful ministry, which again honors the Lord. There must be a revival in the practice of New Testament repentance among the ministers of the Lord *and* a compassion for those who have fallen to get them back into the race of ministry again. Remember: The *calling* is perpetual (Romans 11:29).

45. What About Church Membership?

The practice of *church membership* has polarized in the last fifty years or so. On the one side, administrative accounting of church people within a local church or denomination has degenerated into equating administrative membership with those in the church who are *saved,* or supposed to be. As the charismatic renewal got under way (1965–1983), there was a tendency to abort anything that smacked of religious tradition; one of these things happened to be administrative church membership. This, along with many other things, was considered nonbiblical and was discarded by many.

Many things in the Christian environment quickly become polarized and ultimately have need to be brought into spiritual *balance.* I believe this is the case with *church membership.* Just as strict rules and administrative accounting are necessary for the accounting of tithes and offerings, it is also necessary to keep an administrative handle on the membership of the church for good reasons, such as communication with those who have placed their souls under the spiritual guidance and oversight of the church and with those who need to be notified about Christian services and ministry within the church community.

In the balance of things, there is no similarity between administrative membership and a person's current spiritual status (lifestyle) with the Lord. As each convert or transfer member is placed upon a proper track of Christian discipleship, he will be able to maintain his true relationship with the Lord. The fact that someone's name appears on an administrative list should not in any way confuse his *administrative* membership with his spiritual relationship with Jesus, any more than one's name appearing on the mailing list of some catalog company makes him a part owner of that same company.

For planning, service opportunities, and purposes of gaining consensus within the daily life of the church, it is both expedient and wise to have a ready reference as to who is or is not a viable part of the local church community.

46. How to Receive Converts and/or Members into Your Church

Somewhere in the process, there needs to be a *public* affirmation, whether the new members are received at the end of an altar call, upon completion of membership qualification training, or upon being water baptized. This public declaration of covenant relationship is important, both personally and corporately (the local body of Christ). Many churches wait until some type of *confirmation* training is completed before they recognize people into membership or water baptize them; many other churches feel the urgency to accomplish water baptism as soon after conversion as is practical.

I feel that under the present stress of what I call "American cultural Christianity," the newly converted must have a simple but thorough definition of what it really means to become born again. Today there is so much religious misperception about what being a Christian really means. Once people understand this, they can truly follow Jesus in water baptism.

However, for the most part in American churches, the predominance of new members comes through transferring membership from other churches (the reason for this is the fact that so little evangelism is being practiced by them). This source of new members has its own set of problems. Unless a family has newly moved into your area, their transferring membership to your church ought to be under spiritual suspect; that is, they should possess a spiritually valid reason for changing churches. Many times it is because of a problem, a problem they have within themselves that they have not dealt with. Many times it is because they have a disagreement with the leadership of the former church, and rather than deal with it, they choose to leave. These problems will be automatically transferred into your ministry or church family (like catching a cold).

I always inquired of those who desired to transfer membership from a sister church as to their reason(s) for leaving the other church. Did they gain the blessing of their former pastor as they left? I had them return and correct the problem/relationship before I would receive their request for membership in our church. I always called the pastor to verify that this was accomplished. Then I would call their pastor to verify that all was well. And when disgruntled people would leave our fellowship, I would call the church they approached (if I knew) for new membership and discuss the matter with the pastor.

More often than not, people move their membership to another church because they lack commitment to the vision. Some people join a church to get in on a new fad. These people are not spiritually stable and can never really commit to your vision. Many people transfer church membership when *their* problem is exposed; rather than deal with the issue, they just feel "led of the Lord." You do not want or need these additional unsolved problems added to your ministry. Usually, all these people come in the *front* door of your church and head directly out the *back* door; this is hardly what I call church growth. One never knows what genes an *adopted* child has, but you can rest assured that you know how your own children (converts) will act—just like you!

Receiving transfer memberships is best done by having them indoctrinated into your beliefs, vision, and ministry. Then have them state their commitment to the vision and authority of the house in a public service or have them sign a covenant that states their understanding and loyalty to the vision of the house. A real *team player* always wears his team uniform with pride.

47. How to Orient New Members into the Church

As a good, well-rounded education precedes a successful life, so a proper (time and content) orientation makes for fruitful church members. They must understand who God is, who they are, and that the devil is real. They should know what the church believes and why. It is imperative that they are familiar with the vision of the house and their potential place within that vision. They must be inspired with the fact that they are leaders (people of influence) and not just *members* (benchwarmers).

Converts and transfer members must be placed upon a *training* track that will form their characters and release their giftings, as well as train them in the fundamentals of Christian leadership. This training should be systematic, exciting, and long enough in duration to transform them into stable lifestyles of servanthood, which will provide not only confidence but also a real sense of ownership in the vision of the local church. Bible study and learning to pray are imperative, but consistent nurturing with a hands-on practicum of Christian service is vital, as it is in the formative years of raising children.

Another important aspect to maintaining *healthy* members is the aspect of affirmation. As with your children, the acknowledging of their presence, worth, and place in your life is a vital part of belonging to the family, so it is with each member of the church family. This is best accomplished openly and publicly before the congregation.

The key to a healthy church is based upon the fervor for evangelism within the body of Christ. Every believer, with his new nature, is excited about seeing souls saved, especially the lost ones he personally knows. The best instruction for leading souls to Christ is by doing it; practical mentoring will assist those who have grown cold in their evangelistic fervor to return to their basic function as believers.

When this element of spirituality becomes the norm, the pastor will have those sheep that are truly birthed into the vision of the house, and a truly efficient method of discipleship will be necessary, for the growth will demand it. The principle of twelve is highly suggested to conserve all the new growth.

48. How to Disciple New Converts and Members

Jesus' last command to His disciples and from them to all believers down through time was to win the world and then to teach them all things, that is, to disciple them. But first you need to retain your new additions before you can properly disciple them. Presently, the attrition rate for all additions into your church is 80 percent. For every 100 members you gain, only 20 will remain with you. This is an inexcusable percentage. What if your banking establishment had the same record: out of every $100 your church deposited, only $20 was credited to your account? Intolerable! Obviously, there is a *better* way to conserve your membership. Your conservation process needs to have an efficient follow-up and an effective discipleship strategy.

In every meeting where an invitation to receive Christ is given, the new converts should be taken to a private room, and their new experience in the Lord should be verified several times, giving them the assurance of their commitment to the Lord. Each one is counseled by a responsible leader, and his phone number and address are received, with the promise given to him that he will receive follow-up. The convert is called by the counselor in 24 hours and visited at his home within 72 hours, and there he is invited to attend the next small group meeting.

The new believer is baptized and needs to be enrolled on a discipleship track that is of sufficient duration to see him stabilized and plugged into the church. I would highly recommend again the principle of twelve strategy, as it uses a continuous and spirit-building track of nine months. By the end of this time, the new member is trained in the fundamentals of the faith and is also challenged and equipped in leadership and begins a small group of his own. This track perpetuates the vital process of evangelism, while at the same time lowering the attrition rate to a low, low 20 percent.

49. How to Discipline Church Members

Every form of discipline brought forth in our lives has the positive effect of strengthening our lives, whether it is the discipline of training or the discipline of correction. As much as effective mentoring is really lacking in most churches providing a hands-on approach to learning every facet of our faith, needed correction is just as critical and, without question, less employed than true mentoring and teaching. The Scriptures are replete with instructions for loving correction, but most real pastors find confrontation (of any sort) hard to accomplish, and usually it is put off until it is too late, or it is never employed. We all know that when a problem appears, the spiritual thing to do is to deal with it, settle the issue, and move on to greater works in the Lord.

As we deal with this issue, I want to maintain a balance between insufficient correction and abusive or excessive correction. Matthew 18:15–35 is a good basis for implementing church discipline. First and foremost, discipline begins with a personal, one-on-one encounter. Every believer is commanded to approach another believer about any scriptural attitude or behavior affecting either one of them; it remains a personal and private matter between two brothers in the Lord, with the settlement of the difference not affecting the local church and remaining a private matter between the two brothers. The rule is simply that the offended believer should seek out privately the believer who has caused the offense to seek for forgiveness and reconciliation.

The second step in church discipline, should it become necessary (99 percent of the time the problem is totally resolved by lovingly implementing the first step), is to approach the person of offense in the company of two spiritually mature witnesses (arbitrators) and seek resolution to the offense. Normally, this step will produce the solution and bring peace to the situation; however, if this step fails, Jesus has given us the third step.

This third step is to bring to the *church* the unresolved problem (1 Corinthians 5:1–13), with both parties present and the set man (pastor) announcing the verdict that the uncooperative person is to be considered a "heathen," that is, to be treated as a lost person. As a lost person, he is no longer a member of the body of Christ and will be treated as such. He is to be prayed for and compassionately witnessed to as a lost person; however, he is not to be fellowshipped with as a believer by the local believers, meaning he loses his *peer* privileges of social and spiritual fellowship.

A word of warning: Following this step when it is called for can precipitate two problems. First, if you have not taught this principle in the church and set it in as an operating precedent for your church, the family and close friends of the guilty person may have trouble with the apparent austerity of this step taught by Jesus and may cause problems within the fellowship and/or simply leave. Secondly, some of the faithful members may overreact and "freeze out" the guilty party, not recognizing or accepting him later when he does repent and desires to be restored to the local body of Christ (2 Corinthians 2:1–11). The leadership must be sensitive in these situations to handle directly either of these scenarios.

I can give personal testimony as a pastor for years of the strength this adds to your church. Church discipline used according to Jesus' words actually brings revival to the local church every time, especially the third step. God honors His Word.

50. How to Cope with People Leaving the Church

Every pastor continually faces the fact of people leaving his church for any number of reasons, both good and bad. This leaving the church scenario, for any reason, invariably causes a mild trauma. As the undershepherd of the flock, you have invested time, love, and relationship in the care and nurturing of your members, so it is naturally depressing when you face their leaving. You lose members through death and because of employment changes, as well as from a multitude of selfish reasons on their part. These reasons are such things as all their friends are leaving the church, they are facing (usually causing) a personality conflict, or they are not getting their own way about something. The list of petty issues is endless.

The first thing you must do after praying is not to try to talk them out of their decision, but to check your own heart and be certain that any conflict, real or imagined, has been honestly and lovingly dealt with. Next, you should stand against the wiles of the enemy as he tries to give you a sense of rejection. Pastors cannot function well when they submit to rejection and must continually guard their hearts against potential hurt.

Remember: They are not *your* members to begin with;

they belong to God. You are accountable only for being the best undershepherd you are called to be. As stated above, the average church today continually loses 80 percent of those who come into the church, but this percentage can be reduced significantly by focusing on winning the lost (the newly saved are so easily bonded to you and your vision and your spiritual authority) and then properly discipling them (have a long enough track so they can buy into the vision of the house). This greatly reduces the possibility of those who would leave for petty, selfish reasons.

You have no reason (or right) to take personally anyone's leaving, for good or bad reasons; you are a steward over your local church, and God is the landlord. When people realize that they belong to and are responsible to God, they automatically begin to grow in spiritual maturity (keeping their hearts and minds on serving others, not on petty, selfish whims).

Keep in mind several things: The only string that you should *tie* people to your ministry with is the cord of *love!* They also need to be trained in the meaning and practice of covenant and commitment. They must be told that leaving will not solve their problems, because most of their problems are within; and they will most certainly carry their problems with them wherever they go. The right thing for them to do is to solve the problem first, and then, if necessary, leave (chances are good they will not).

Treat "your" people wisely, like you handle money.

Don't hoard them zealously, but rather invest them (and all their giftings) into the kingdom of God (the *good* bank) and watch with pleasure the high return from your good stewardship, namely the joy of their increase in the kingdom of God.

51. How to Avoid Crisis Management Syndrome

One sure way to have an unproductive ministry and become one of the growing numbers of pastors that suffer burnout is to become snared with a ministry style of crisis management. Crisis management is the dealing with situations that you have let get out of hand and that are now ready to fall apart or blow up. Remember: Problems are normal, but crises are not. The constant rise of crises is a telltale sign of several possible defects in your life ministry: procrastination, a lack of strategy, no effective goals set, lack of prayer/fasting, a neglect of the Spirit gift of discerning, or a lack of "anticipation." Failure here gets the same results as when you fail to perform preventive maintenance on your car (you see these kinds of people on the side of the highway all the time: out of fuel, needing a jump start, or unable to fix a flat tire because of no workable spare tire), and these same people seem to have one "road crisis" after another.

Many ministers of the Gospel go from crisis to crisis until they are overcome with discouragement or ministerial burnout—all because of what I call "spiritual dissipation." They are letting themselves be controlled by circumstances, instead of taking control of the circumstances in their ministries.

Let me review with you how to take control of your circumstances. Without an adequate vision of the house in place (i.e., concise, clear, challenging vision that is well articulated by you and attractively posted around your "plant"), your ministry will never get off the ground or is certain to drift. You will do what many do: give priority to the immediate duty of that day and the rest is history; the domino effect starts with one urgent demand following another, until you use the whole day putting out a few fires and accomplish zero of your God-given vision.

Again, procrastination is a ministry killer caused by mental laziness; and just like with physical laziness your muscles get atrophied, so will your work ethic. Putting off the hard or distasteful things and letting them slide will cause your ability to accept and deal with challenges to become atrophied. This syndrome is overcome only by spiritual discipline, prayer, and fasting. If you do not deal with this, your life and ministry will drift into self-centeredness and remain unfulfilled. Just as with physical exercise, only a daily regimen of prioritizing your time and responsibilities will overcome this sin.

I cannot emphasize enough for you to have a clear, challenging vision, but without implementing a strategy and obtainable goals, you will just wander around and accomplish pitifully little of your potential. *Write* down your vision, listing each aspect in clear, concise form that is easily memorized by you and your people. If you use bulletins for your services, have it permanently printed on one side. Post it in an attractive form in the vestibules of your church plant. Then with your team devise an efficient strategy implementing each segment of the vision. Then prayerfully set attainable goals that will afford easy measurement in weekly, monthly, and yearly increments.

Remember that goals are challenges, and if they are not always attained on schedule, they can easily be reset. The main idea is to be able to recognize the progress of the vision, which is vital for good morale and required for good stewardship.

Every pastor is ill-equipped until he has coveted the gift of the Holy Spirit that Paul describes as discerning of spirits. God wants His leaders to choose spiritually qualified people to work with them in the vision of the house. Too many pastors lack discerning as they assign people to their parts of the vision of the house. Discerning is not "the gift of suspicion"; it is discerning of someone's spirit and character. A man may have the right gifting but may lack in character, allowing him to do damage to your team and/or the vision. Everyone on your team must have orally confirmed your place as leader and desire to relate to your ministry as a son in the house.

Finally, a man of God needs to be able to *anticipate.* This is not to provoke worry or invoke a "spooky spirituality." Before you have experience (all of us find ourselves there) in the next phase of the vision, allow the Holy Spirit to nudge you and prepare you for what is about to happen (not "could happen"—that is unbelief). This will keep your soul from being defeated or discouraged.

The rule summarized: Get the vision from God. Keep it before God. Then work like you are supposed to do it all, and when it succeeds, give God all the glory!

52. How to Face Confrontation and Stay Positive

Confrontation is much like the weather. We appreciate the gentle rains that are beneficial and comforting; however, as much as we realize that we need the moisture, most of us dislike a clashing thunderstorm. So it is with pastoring people. People can be fun and are appreciated until the inevitable occasion comes when you have to give them a needed reproof or rebuke so they can get back on track and stay there. Confrontations, like thunderstorms, are a necessary factor of life.

You must allow the Holy Spirit to help you during these times, allowing Him to manage your <u>attitudes</u> and the <u>methods</u> of confrontation during these times. Your *attitude* is primary during confrontation; you should employ the fruit of the Spirit:

- Remember that the goal of all confrontation is *restoration;* it is never vindictive during correction, nor is it a time to vent your frustrations. If you are enjoying the confrontation, you are in a wrong attitude; employ the Holy Spirit fruit of gentleness, which in reality is "others' consciousness."
- Confrontation must be done in authority and truth,

but not while you are angry. Wait until you have control of your emotions and the situation; here employ the fruit of meekness.
- Confrontation is temporary, but relationships are permanent; here use the fruit of love.
- Confrontation requires courage to bring to the light the truth to the lives of those being confronted; employ the fruit of goodness (moral integrity).
- Be sure that you are in an attitude of true accountability yourself before you begin the process; here employ the fruit of temperance (self-control).
- Condemnation has no place during confrontation; use the fruit of peace.

The *methods* you use to employ confrontation must also be godly:

- Timing is crucial. Do not succumb to either procrastination or impulse, as both are in the realm of the soul.
- If at all possible, confrontation must be accomplished in privacy. Even when dealing with a group, their collective privacy must be protected. There may come a time when the truth or authority is challenged and an open rebuke becomes necessary, but this is not the norm.
- Do not abuse or wrongly use your authority structure; lines of delegated authority must be clearly in

place. In other words, are you the one who is supposed to be conducting the confrontation?

- Make certain you have beforehand all the facts and time sequences concerning the scenario.
- Never end the session with negative criticism (which is usually a necessary part of confrontation), but rather end with a positive plan or suggestion, which may even require a ministry change.

53. How to Maintain Relationship Within the Local Church

It is one thing to make friends, but it is another thing to *keep* them. The pastorate has a multifaceted responsibility in this regard, but the overriding factor in permanent relationships is *integrity*. Integrity is strictly a character/heart issue. Times, conditions, purposes and plans all change with the progress of time; in fact, everything will eventually change, except the issue of your integrity.

Integrity can best be defined as the "consistent manifestation of Christ's character." Anybody can be nice or honest or loving for a season, but a lifestyle of character becomes your integrity.

A lack of integrity results in people being used and ultimately trashed. True relationships are not expendable, and only true integrity can weather emotional storms, deep disappointments, and even acts of sedition (Judas Iscariot) in keeping with Christ's love.

Integrity never comes to us "assembled and ready for use." It is more like a quilted comforter, requiring a painstaking, lengthy process to achieve its final beauty. It is even said of Jesus, "Though he were a Son, yet learned he obedience by the things he suffered" (Hebrews 5:8). Integrity is crafted within us by God's love and is ever ongoing. Integrity has no agenda; it is without guile. Love, trust, and a firm belief in the person fosters true relationships that will open the door for leaders to lead faithfully and followers to consistently follow.

Starting a church or assuming the post of pastor at a church does not make you the people's *pastor.* Only the outworking of Psalm 23 between a pastor and his people (always on an individual or family basis) produces relationships that will sustain the vision of the house. Sharing in the joy of a birth or a long awaited salvation, performing a marriage, or sharing crises of death, job loss, or divorce in the family allows you to enter into real relationships.

Handshaking, name-memorizing, and halfhearted smiles are but mere professional services in the ministry; only when personalities are stretched and the garment of life is turned to the "seamy side" are you entering into a pastoral relationship. Your age, experience, and education are all helpful, but they are not necessary to form a relationship. Remember: Relationships formed within your church/ministry are eternal.

Paul's reminder to Timothy to treat the older men with the respect given to a father, to treat the older women in the church as mothers, to treat the young men as brothers, and to treat the young women as sisters (this not only helps to eliminate the lust factor but also opens up a place for women in the vision of the house) will provide the necessary integrity, morality, ethics, and love essential for relationships to be formed and ongoing in the local church.

54. Understanding Peer Relationships

The truth that all men are created equal before God is a simple truth that has been idealized by the American Constitution, though never really realized in real life because of carnal hearts; yet it is still pursued for the good of all. Many people in the church in the pursuit of this axiom have allowed themselves to crowd out another pertinent truth pertaining to healthy relationships in the kingdom of God.

God has given to us *peer relationships* as a guardian principle. Yet there are those, some of whom are godly men, who fail to comprehend this principle, to the detriment of kingdom peace and progress. For example, the church still vacillates on the distinction between clergy and laity. The conflict is a result of confusing value with service. Every soul is of equal *value* before God; however, God Himself calls and gives gifts to certain men to *lead* and other men to *follow.* One distinction between the leader and the follower is the placement and stewardship of spiritual authority with its complementary responsibility used to start and sustain a God-given vision.

Jesus Himself employed this governmental and visionary truth of *peer relationships* with His twelve disciples. The Twelve were not worth more to Him than the multitudes of people, but they were called out to perform specific responsibilities and were given commensurate authority to see them accomplished. In that role, they were *peers.* Peers *are people with similar, designated responsibilities who have a viable and specific need to share in a relationship together in order to be able to perform their duties with more excellence.*

Jesus further exemplified the necessity of *peer* relationships in that He also had His inner three within His twelve disciples. Of course, He could never be construed as playing favorites, but this inner group demonstrated the keen sense of reality and need of *peer* levels among men. Peerage has nothing to do with a varied worth of souls before God—much less before men—but it is essential for ministerial responsibility to be effective among leaders and followers.

A common example of this kind of relationship is found in the family. Parents do not discuss everything with their children; they would be remiss if they discussed their financial planning or their sexuality with their six-year-old son and three-year-old daughter. This is certainly not a question of value or rights, but a simple matter of leaders and followers.

With the reality and validity of peerage established, let us consider ways to enhance the need of specific relationships of the leadership within a church. One is to have clearly recognized areas of responsibilities. Secondly, it will be obvious that those with the greater responsibilities will of necessity spend more time with the pastor to accomplish the vision. This is not a matter of favoritism, but of team players that are responsible to get the job done.

There was no revealed jealousy between Jesus' inner circle of three and the larger group of twelve or for that matter, the seventy; the only problem that arose was when James and John wanted a greater *value* placed upon them over the rest of the Twelve.

There is also a subtle but important distinction of the communication within peer groups. Pastors and pastors' wives, especially in smaller churches, breach the rule of peer relationships by doing what I call "peering down." Because of the lack of peers in a small fellowship and the pressing need to have relationships, the leaders in these situations start confiding with their *followers* (placing them in unwarranted and undesignated responsibilities of leadership); the result is that the followers are placed under spiritual pressures they were never called to or equipped to handle. The end result (always close at hand) of this breach of peer relationships is spiritual overkill and/or fostering pride within a novice (Paul warns against this), causing an overfamiliarity that usually results in rebellion or disillusionment.

This is why pastors' fellowship meetings and mentoring groups that meet on a regular basis are so necessary for peer relationships; they serve as pressure relief valves for ministers and their wives who are beset with problems but have little or no fellowship with their peers (fellow pastors). These meetings also offer a platform for sharing and mentoring within a peer environment.

Proof of all this *peer* stuff can be seen at every mixed gathering of people. Men invariably "peer" to men and ladies to ladies. In fact, musicians will somehow find each other and group together, as will mothers and even motorcycle riders. Peer relationship is an undeniable part of our created makeup and ministry. It is absolutely essential in the formation of relationships in the local church.

55. How to Be Transparent

Jesus was quite clear about the depraved nature of godless men and the lingering effect it has even after we have been redeemed. He remarked that men loved darkness rather than light because their deeds were evil. The more we let the Word wash us, the more light we desire to walk in.

These natural compulsions to "hunker in the shadows" are present not only in new converts, but also in all believers, even those in the ministry. Keeping our past in the shadows is one of our greatest hindrances to a vibrant ministry. The less we think we have to hide, the more real we can become to others.

Jesus had no sin, and He walked among men as an open book, hiding nothing. He is your example for a lifestyle of openness. There is no reason for you as a minister of the Lord to walk around with shadows in your soul. Any shame remaining after the blood has cleansed your soul from sin just serves as a signpost to prompt you to humility and thanksgiving, and as a prod to walk in holiness. Talking about your past is not usually your initial conversation with people; at the same time, your past should not be shrouded in guilt, for God's forgiveness changes your shame into gratitude. Even trying to hide the dumb things you have done is, in all reality, an evidence of pride. Don't try to build your ministerial image on a *false* perfection.

Just as bragging on a past life of degradation is really magnifying the sin—not the Savior—so, too, does allowing your past to keep you in a dungeon of secrecy shackle you from becoming "real." Your lack of reality before men produces suspicion and sets up a realm of mistrust that stymies any real chance of building relationships.

By now you will agree that becoming *transparent* with people, especially your peers, is not the easiest thing to do. In all honesty, it has been, without exception, the hardest lesson I have had to learn. On the other hand, discretion does not call for you on your first encounter with people to just let it all hang out! Relationships are built gradually upon a foundation of trust as each person becomes real.

I have found the greatest impact on people that enables them to receive my teaching comes when I have been candid and honest with those to whom I am ministering. It levels the playing field to where everyone feels able to enter in and inventory his life and feels free to openly acknowledge and act upon a needed change in his life or ministry. I often incorporate a personal testimony of my "dumbness" or a victory in an area in my life as I seek to build relationships with those I am mentoring.

Honesty and openness are essential tools in leading people, affording rapport and trust to be established and accelerated between them. Transparency includes the fact you can honestly acknowledge the giftings that God has placed within your life and use them with confidence. It is pride, not transparency, when you deny or belittle those gift(s) from God. If you can sing or preach well, it is false humility (a lie) to say you cannot. You are being transparent when you, with all honesty, can realize that you can do something better than someone else, while at the same time acknowledge, without feeling belittled, that someone else can do something better than you.

Transparency is being open and peer-sensitive while at the same time allowing zero focus on you (pride). The more your people can identify with you, the easier it is for them to receive your ministry.

56. The Place of Mentoring Within the Ministry

Mentoring has nearly become a lost art. Mentoring is the time-proven method for transmitting wisdom and knowledge through a one-on-one or one-to-a-small-group relationship.

The fashionable "how to" conferences and books available today simply do not help most people. Not that they are not good—but they have a common fallacy; namely, the book or conference shares with you a new method which may be very good, but all that *you* receive is the knowledge of the method. You do not receive the anointing the person has who discovered this great method. Example: A pastor develops a great way to grow your church. You attend the conference he holds to explain his method, and you buy his book. You go back to your church and follow all the instructions to the "T." To your disillusionment, your success does not even compare to his. What went wrong? You don't have his anointing! You cannot *learn* anointing by attending a meeting or reading a book; it is only bestowed by God. And a method without the anointing to operate it is like a kiss over the telephone: you hear it, but you don't have it.

Mentoring provides a one-on-one, hands-on impartation

that ensures not only the transferring of information, but also the anointing that is essential to see it come to fruition. Mentoring provides both the receiving of and implementing of the vision that God gives to all His called. It also provides a close relationship to ensure counsel in the areas of your life that need grooming, such as family relationships, financial stewardship, ethics, and morale.

Mentoring is the age-old system of a father passing on to his son the *secrets* of their family business. In a mentoring relationship, time is taken to guide you into fruitfulness, and that experience and wisdom are passed on from one generation to the next.

It is to your advantage to seek out that person who is willing and competent to receive you as a true *son* as you submit your life and ministry to his godly expertise and grace. Like a father, he will love you and give you an impartation of life and ministry that will provide the heritage and the posterity God desires for you and your ministry.

57. How to Delegate

As your ministry grows, the related details of it will soon consume too much of your time and obscure your gifting(s). As your vision matures and comes into fruition, you must acquire proper helpers to come alongside and assist you. You will need those who will serve as volunteers and those who will become full-time ministers. These people must have clear and complete understanding of their respective responsibilities and the authority necessary to complete their task(s).

Many pastors do not reach their potential and realize the vision God has given to them because they are perfectionists or are weak in discerning the spiritual place and potential their would-be helpers should have. The perfectionist does not see nor is willing to release people to their potential and spends all his time doing everything, wasting time doing what he is not good at, which keeps his ministry from growing. The person who loves everybody and lets everyone do what he wants (most of whom desire to have a platform for their own agendas) finds his efforts to do his vision dissipated.

God calls pastors to *lead,* not *do,* the vision He has called them to. The larger it grows, the less of the hands-on work he gets to do, because his time is consumed with receiving and communicating the vision's strategy as it progresses daily. The first thing you must do is thoroughly grasp the vision. Next, you must prioritize the duties of the vision. With this done, you must select, train, release, and measure the accomplishments of all whom God gives you to get the job done.

When a job within the vision is clearly defined with both the responsibilities and the authority needed, let God lead you in the selection of that individual. Discerning must be exempt from pettiness and personal prejudices. Discerning will clearly point out ability, character, and the person's ability to be a team player in your vision. In 1 Timothy, the third chapter reminds us that this person must have a good reputation, both within the church as well as outside it. It is better to have just a part-time volunteer than a fully paid staff member who will cause you more pain and disruption within the vision.

Every leader must learn from Moses. Doing his vision was wearing him and the people out until he listened to his father-in-law and delegated a necessary but time-consuming facet of the whole vision of God. He took those in varied levels of responsibility and delegated each one within his ability. As Moses did, you will do best by your people and for the vision by using the ones God has given to you, but if no one is qualified, then you can look outside the congregation to accomplish the task. "Homegrown" tastes better; these already have your doctrinal background and are in the vision.

Every true leader must begin immediately praying for and seeking out someone who will ultimately take his place. A true leader always works himself out of a job, just as Jesus trained and used the Twelve. God gives to you and every leader those who will responsibly and with fruitfulness follow you, but for them to stay with you, they must have a *delegated* part. Remember: You can delegate anything but the vision God has placed in your life.

58. How to Get Your People to Follow

Most pastors at some point in their ministries despair over their people not *following* the plan, the vision, the program, etc. The underlying cause for a few could be that they are in the wrong place (church), they have not understood the vision of the house, or they have not dealt with their carnal attitudes. However, the majority of the time that people are not following is because of the fact that they are *not* being led. When people or animals are left without competent leadership, they have no focus and soon stop and ultimately disperse.

A pastor who can't get his congregation to see the need does not always need to give another teaching; the pastor must *lead* the way. Leadership is not limited to telling or instruction; leading is best accomplished by lifestyle. A good leader informs and instructs his followers by demonstration, by presence, and by passion. He will do it, and he will do it before and with his followers; but his leadership will only be successful according to his passion. He can only impart what he is. Hype, hypocrisy, and hollering soon turn off a would-be follower and bring an end to his following.

This is why any announcement made in church is only as valid as the passion and authority of the one who makes it. If you want your church to really be involved with something, you must make the announcement. Math teachers teach math; they do not make bankers.

Your people will follow you to the edge and beyond if they know you are leading and if what you are saying lines up with the passion of your performance. You can lead your people into an effective lifestyle of prayer only if you yourself are passionate about it. People need teaching on giving offerings, but your passionate demonstration and testimony will make a 95 percent difference in the size of any given offering you truly act out in your role as *leader.*

Years ago, my congregation drifted into a noisy and an altogether unaware attitude of the presence of God in our preservice time. As I had opportunity, I mentioned this and began to publicly demonstrate my passion (for His presence) during our preservice time; the congregation simply *followed* my example, almost to a person, in a matter of a month. It did not take chiding and reprimand to get the results I felt were necessary, just the demonstration of my passionate desire for His presence during this crucial time before and as each service began.

The passionate pronouncement of real vision and vital issues acted out by the leader will always get his followers moving closely behind him. This primary privilege/ responsibility of real leaders must be used in Holy Spirit wisdom to further the cause of the kingdom of God.

59. Maintaining Balance Within Christian Ministry

Each local church will generally have the tendency to "pendulum-ize" (go to the left or right of the intended teaching of Scripture). This happens with our doctrine, our worship, and with our service to the Lord (Christian ministry). Some congregations are taught only to acquire the fruit of the Holy Spirit (Galatians 5:22–23) and build a Christlike character in their personal lives. On the other hand, other congregations are taught to seek foremost the gifts of the Holy Spirit (1 Corinthians 12:7–11) and to minister in the power of God as they carry out the Great Commission.

It should be obvious that both are necessary and should be acquired in a harmonious *balance.* Ministry and serving without the character of Christ (holiness) is both ineffective and inexcusable, just as serving the Lord without His power (gifts) dissipates into a mere carnal effort that proves to be both exhausting and ineffective. Since the Lord requires both, He expects us to minister with both as we live our daily lives of serving and representing Him to the world.

It is the pastor's responsibility to see that every believer is taught and coached in the *balance* of character and power. Each believer should be encouraged to develop the nine (the *number* of the Holy Spirit) "fruit" of the Spirit and the nine gifts of the Spirit simultaneously, lest they become so heavenly minded, they are of no earthly use, or again, attempt to move in spiritual power without the grace and compassion of God's true character, leaving those ministered to with nothing but the stench of ego.

In the language of today's church, the nine "fruit" of the Holy Spirit can best be stated as the following: The fruit of the Spirit *is* (singular—one source) godly love, like the sun shining equally on all, without end or provocation. Joy is from the root word *grace;* therefore, it is the effect of grace upon our lives. Peace is the *foundation* of our experience with Christ; we either have it in place, or everything else becomes precarious and without substance. Longsuffering is enduring patience wisely in place without deference to other circumstances. Gentleness is the response of kindness and concern to every provocation; it is turning the other cheek. Goodness has to do with the integrity of our morals. Faith is not a substantive, but an adjective describing our fortitude of example despite the circumstances involved. Meekness is best translated as "teachableness." Temperance best describes our *self-control.*

Today the nine gifts of the Holy Spirit are best described in the three areas of ministry: (1) *revelation:* word of knowledge (facts of past and present), word of wisdom (divine application of facts and truth), and discerning of spirits (plural—God, angels, man, good or evil); (2) *power:* miracles (God intervening by removing time or creating essentials), faith, and healings (plural—gifting within ministry); and (3) *vocal:* prophesying (the Holy Spirit speaking immediately through man), tongues (words from the Holy Spirit through man to God, either devotionally or ministry, accompanied by authority), and interpretation of tongues, which makes it tantamount to prophecy.

60. The Place and Position of Authority and Anointing

Authority and anointing are both from God. Although they are different in purpose, they can and should work harmoniously in your life. Authority is the force of righteous order emanating from Father God. All authority is from God and is only delegated. Authority is the sovereign rule of God's will in all matters, both spiritual and natural. The realm and context of authority is called government.

In ministry you are delegated authority, and it is exercised in the context of God's grace as "divine right." Authority in the ministry is manifested through or by the office of your calling. A man may have the call of God upon his life to be a pastor, but he has no viable authority (only anointing) to accomplish that work until he is set into the office of pastor (within a certain place). Along with the authority resident in the office of the pastor, God prescribes certain responsibilities and privileges. When the pastor preaches a sermon, it comes forth with the authority that is resident within that office, making it effective and efficacious (authoritative). It is also true that when a man leaves the office of that pastorate (a certain local church), he no longer has the authority held by that office.

Anointing is the grace of God's presence granted upon the gift (fivefold calling) and/or giftings (God-endowed talents and skills). The anointing can and should be present continually upon these endowments. You never have to work up anointing, like winding a clock or waiting for a wind to arise to fly a kite. The indwelling of the Holy Spirit is present in you, endowing the anointing to operate from your spirit just as easily as your mind operates in your knowing (your name, etc.). The only way to stop your resident anointing is by leaving your consecration through sin(ning).

A lost person may have a gift for playing the violin and do so with great skill, but without the Spirit and consecration, he has no anointing. A spiritual man can have a moderate gifting for singing, and to the proportion of the gifting, it will carry the anointing. Anything that is consecrated to God should carry the anointing (Leviticus states that all the articles of the tabernacle, when properly consecrated with oil, became anointed by God; the personal pronouns changed from neuter to masculine). When a pastor preaches a message—according to the revelation and consecration it carries—it is anointed, as well as the anointing upon his preaching gift.

Authority and anointing are distinct, yet complementary. Authority is resident in the office (official) of God (in Jeremiah's day there were many "official" [recognized by the king] prophets, but only Jeremiah had authority delegated from God). Anointing is resident upon the person's giftings and works that he consecrates to the service of the Lord. Authority is delegated and resident in God's official place of the call(ing); anointing is personal and based upon one's character and consecration to God.

61. The Purpose and Practice of Affirmation

One of the most important aspects of ministry (and of family life) is the extending of *affirmation.* Its neglect is usually because of ignorance on our part.

Affirmation is the positive, announced recognition of value and worth held by the authority figure in your immediate life or ministry. Its importance is usually overlooked and supplanted by negative reports and criticism. Its absence has the same effect in the spiritual realm as does a total vitamin deficiency in your body: you are weak and listless and struggle to go on because you are not consciously aware of the problem. Another illustration is the effect that a compliment has on attitude and self-worth. Many who are emotionally half-starved because of a self-projected status of low self-worth respond to a compliment as a kid does when he is offered candy. In fact, many people will unconsciously or even consciously strive, to the "door" of sin, to earn a compliment.

One reason that affirmation is misunderstood and so lacking in relationships is the fact that affirmation is not supposed to be earned. A baby is loved and welcomed into his family without having to do anything to earn his place as a member of his family. Affirmation has to do with who we *are,* not with what we have *done;* it is based upon our person, not our performance.

Blessing, ordination, and reward should come to us as a result (because) of affirmation. Affirmation is the personal recognition of someone that opens the door of acceptance, definition, understanding, and confidence in the relationship existing between a husband and a wife, a parent and a child, or a mentor and the person he is mentoring.

Affirmation must be as public and vocal as privacy permits; mental acceptance is of no more value than an unspoken compliment. Relationships either never gel or actually diminish when affirmation is neglected. Affirmation can never just be "understood"; it must be spoken and actively demonstrated. Just like a pregnant woman must give birth to her child, so must true affirmation come forth in word and demonstration.

Having said this, let me say that most pastors have not affirmed adequately their own wives into their ministries. As they are one in marriage, so they are one in the ministry; their roles may be different, but they are one in vision and purpose. Most pastors' wives have risen to their place and potential in ministry only to the level of affirmation from their husbands. The same is also true with each person on the staff.

How do you perform affirmation? You vocalize clearly, explicitly, and lovingly your conviction of your appreciation for and your understanding of others' worth; you do it sincerely, acknowledging your full gratitude to God for them and their place in your life and ministry. Then you lay hands on them, transferring the blessing and recognizing the Holy Spirit's sealing of this pronouncement.

Most of the time, the dearth of affirmation is so deep within the soul that you will have to vocally reconfirm it (without the ceremony). Affirmation, because it is a vocal operation, must be updated and restated, just as a marriage ceremony does not ensure a healthy relationship without a regular announcement of "I love you."

62. How to Make and Maintain a Church Budget

One of the major problems affecting the local church today is the practice of poor stewardship. Poor stewardship is the usual cause of the lack of funds that plagues many, many churches. There is no way a pastor can become accountable to God and everyone else without the use of a church budget.

Nearly every church I am called to help does not have an operating budget. When I ask to see it, I am usually presented with an expense sheet telling me where the money has been already spent. This (expense sheet) is not a budget. A budget is the formal decision written in a document that pledges to spend a designated amount for each area of the church life and vision and is the formulated needs expected for the year and submitted by the leader of each area of ministry within the church. A budget begins with an accurate assessment of the projected income of the church for that year and a responsible designation of certain monies to be spent for each item qualified to receive money for that year. It makes sense that if you do not know how much money you plan to spend, you will never know if it comes in, nor can you expect for it to come in.

A budget is not only a responsible decision of accurate

spending to be accomplished during the tenure of that budget (usually a year), but it is also the only way a local church can release faith to incorporate God's blessings and assurance that the projected monies will come in. God cannot and will not bless poor stewardship, that is, irresponsible, unaccountable (dishonest) handling of kingdom money.

Of course, there are many computer programs written to assist a church with an easy and complete operation of a church budget. But for the sake of understanding, we will explain the church budget as though you were using a pad and pencil. The first item to be considered is the annual income to be used for the coming year's budget. A record of all the tithes and offerings and designated funds are readily available, or should be. Remember: Faith money is never a credit situation; God deals only with actual funds. God does not heal imaginary diseases, nor does He bless ungodly stewardship. Only after you account for every penny that came in last year can you exercise faith for an increase of money to come into the church.

Your faith can be released based upon your stewardship of growth, that is, on how seriously you employ evangelism (saving souls). Another source of financial growth in the local church is the prayerful teaching of biblical tithing, in which every believer gives 10 percent of his gross income. The national average of tithers in a local church is less than 25 percent. It would be very unfair to increase the budget and expect only one quarter of the members to bear the increased burden. When I pastored, I taught an annual series (on Sunday mornings) on tithing and stewardship; the church never had less than 85 percent of tithers (the other 15 percent were either just coming into the church or just leaving). After several budget makings, you will be more accurate in projecting the increase of the annual income within your church. Each kind of offering you receive in your church should have a place in the budget.

The second thing on your budget sheet will be your assets. This is the inventory of all material property that you own and that is not serving as collateral. This tells you your present worth in property and materials. The assets will become a necessary entity when you need to prepare a financial statement for a lending institution and for acquiring insurance on your church property.

The third item in your budget is your listed liabilities. This is the sum total of all loans still in effect and their monthly payments.

The fourth item in your budget is the expenses. These should be broken down into major categories, with each expense having its own chart of accounts number for easy reference. For example, if you assign utilities a category number of 600, then each separate utility, such as electricity, telephone, gas, water, etc., will have its own chart of accounts number with expansion capabilities. Electricity will be under the 600 account and given a number of 601. The next utility, telephone, will have a number of 610, leaving the numbers 602 to 609 for possible expansion of the 601 electricity category.

Each major division of your expenses should appear with its own category number, according to its assigned priority. I suggest the following priority: ministry (salaries, and benefits given to paid personnel), missions (local benevolence, national, and world), building (loan payments, maintenance, office equipment and supplies, etc.), utilities, transportation, and the list goes on.

One item that is necessary for every budget is the buffer, or emergency fund. Stewardship requires that you do not plan to spend all your income. Each church should seek to set aside money for a buffer and/or for potential emergencies. An immediate goal should be to have enough money set aside to cover a month's operating expenses, should the need ever arrive (often it does). The ultimate goal is to have six months of budgeted income in reserve. The emergency fund does not include new ideas, equipment upgrades, or so-called "spiritual whims." Any change in the present budget requires a formal budget emendation.

Preparing a budget will require a month or two to formulate, but the result will be a responsible handling of God's money, making it possible for faith to be exercised. Everyone will know exactly where the church finances are at any given moment: the monthly income, the monthly outgo, and the balance for the rest of the year of any budgeted item stated. A year-to-date column lets you know if any item is falling within the projected budget allotment. For example, if $1,200 is budgeted for electricity for the year, and in January the bill is only $90, you have $1,110 left for the rest of the year; but in August the bill may be projected for $110, so you are right on target).

One more word: You as pastor will never succeed in operating with a church budget if you personally do not use (properly) a budget for your personal income. You will not be "clean" at church if you don't first bathe at home!

63. How to Maintain Good Financial Records

Financial integrity is based upon more than just reputation and a desire to do well. A church must keep good records of its financial dealings. There are three things that are essential to record keeping: written permission for all expenditures, written receipts for all transactions, and, finally, someone who has been delegated the authority and responsibility to keep the records.

Written permission means that the expenditure is either in the budget or there is a completed form to accomplish the purchase. Vocal okays are soon forgotten, and details become vague. Unauthorized spending will soon result, and then when correction is made, offenses can be taken up because there is no clear proof of the transaction. A church policy can be written to cover standard transactions.

There must be written receipts for each expenditure, which may include a cancelled check (most banks charge extra for this service), a credit card receipt, or a sales receipt that is turned in before a reimbursement can be made or a transaction validated as an official transaction and not a personal one.

Someone must be delegated to care for the recording

of all financial transactions to assure that it is done and done correctly. Many people are very poor record keepers. Some churches employ a CPA firm to do this, but most churches must rely on a volunteer who is both dedicated and knowledgeable in the financial realm. The business side of the church's activities should not ever be allowed to bring suspicion to someone's spiritual integrity, but it must include permanent records to survive the time and integrity tests.

Records must be kept for a safe amount of time, either in a computer format or contained in adequate filing cabinets. These records should be easily accessible and in proper chronological order. The system of record keeping must always be under surveillance so as to improve accuracy and to cut down on superfluous activity and duplication.

64. Financial Reporting

Giving financial reports is as important as keeping financial records. Every tithing member has a legitimate right to be kept abreast of the church's financial status. Oftentimes there will also be those people who do not belong to the church or have some agenda against it who will demand financial information; these persons have no right to any financial information.

The use of discretion as to timing, frequency, and ensuring that every report is user-friendly is of prime importance. A copy of the annual budget as accomplished during the past year can accompany the report of giving sent annually (or quarterly) to each tithing family and is an ideal way to keep the church family abreast of the church's stewardship.

Posting reports or handing them out during the general service times can possibly provoke unnecessary questions that never get answered and/or cause confusion to the uninitiated and uninformed. If a nonmember is serious about becoming a member and has questions concerning finances that may affect his decision to become a part of the church, it is best to deal with these in a private meeting where these matters may be freely discussed. This will remove any doubts or misperceptions he may have about this matter. It will be necessary to inform people of this available counsel in the visitors' guide packet.

Administrative staff meetings are the place to discuss the progress of the budget and the trends of the church's income, as well as specific needs or corrections necessary for sound financial accounting and productive ministry. Another aspect of true accountability is to involve the church's apostolic covering in the financial area of the church. He will have a great girth of experience, as well as helpful financial information and sources for your church.

65. When to Borrow Money

It should be the goal of every local church to become financially solvent and independent. Having proper stewardship and a God-ordained vision are imperative to seeing this accomplished.

Proper stewardship includes the ethical administration and accounting of money, the responsible and adequate teaching of tithing and stewardship to the congregation, and spiritual sensitivity as to when and how to seek outside financing to accomplish this part of the vision. Having godly vision is as important as understanding completely a product before you purchase it. Buying a six-bedroom house before you have any children is not only premature, but it will also not allow other financial priorities to be attained in proper order; on the other hand, being fully aware of your future family's size will assist you in prioritizing your preparations so as to reach your goal. Your vision should be so clear and held with such conviction that it will not change (before the old vision is paid for) and cause a great deal of wasted time and money, as well as morale.

When you are led to process a segment of the ministry's vision and realize that outside financing will be necessary, any lending agency will expect your stewardship to possess a certain amount of savings accumulated to prove your earnestness for that purpose. They will not allow your payment to exceed the prescribed percent of your annual budget (for a building, your note should not exceed more than a quarter of your annual income). You must watch the use of collateral because a lending institution will want all your assets to serve as collateral for the loan, and this could be excessive.

The church will have within its bylaws a group of men (trustees) who are authorized to represent the church in the negotiation of a loan. Men in this office are not necessarily elders, ministers on staff, or decreed to have any spiritual authority within the church.

You may decide to use the process of church bonds in place of making a loan with some agency. You need to be assured that the company you use has a proven success rate and will maintain an ethical and spiritual relationship with *your* people (remember that they are in the business of making money). Know also that with church bonds, there is always the remote possibility that some member of your church may become disenchanted with the ministry and want to opt out of his agreement. Usually the company has this factor built into its procedures, but you need to know this beforehand to preclude any possible problem, slander, or attack on the ministry.

If you are considering a building project with the plan to pay as you go, you need to consider one thing: usually this process will take longer (sometimes much longer) than you initially forecast. The odds are that the people, especially the men coming for Saturday workdays (and their neglected families), will burn out and adversely affect morale and the spiritual revival a new facility carries with it.

Every church dreams of a new building just off the interstate. A high profile is only one consideration in prioritizing your vision. It makes little sense to have your building just off the interstate if it will take a road map to get to it once people get off the interstate highway. How many people driving on the interstate will feasibly become members of your church? Interstate highways are made to cover vast distances; you probably will not have too many interstate (out-of-state) members.

A high profile is good, but adequate, affordable property is a real consideration. Future expansion and adequate parking are real priorities in themselves. Remember: Your church ministry will be the basic drawing factor for your church. The late John Osteen's Oasis of Love in Houston, Texas, is a classic example of this (the old church for many years was in a most unlikely, hard-to-get-to place in town).

66. How to Receive Tithes and Offerings

More opinions reign about this portion of the church service than any other, from an elaborate and official collection to receiving of multiple times to giving to boxes placed in a conspicuous place in the rear of the auditorium.

I believe the Old Testament confirms that the tithe and all offerings are to be dedicated in an act of worship (Deuteronomy 26) and, as such, should be regarded as a portion of all worship accomplished in the church. Several guidelines are suggested. As an act of worship, receiving God's money on His behalf should be conducted in His *holy* presence. God's money is *received* by the church, not collected or taken. As being an act of worship, it should hold that status and not be encumbered with "necessary" announcements, frivolous fellowship, musical distractions, or even testimonies. The servants who receive the money must be discreet during the act of worship and not be conspicuous in the depositing of the tithes and offerings. There is no valid reason why the money should be counted during the rest of the hour of worship; God already knows what has been given, and you can't do a thing about it because your bank is closed until the next business day.

The offering time is a good time to present a clear, brief exhortation as to the scriptural meaning of the act and God's response to it. It is also important as a point of honesty to use the monies received for the *purpose* you told the people that the money was gathered for. If, for example, you are receiving an offering for a missionary or some other guest minister, be certain that every cent is placed in his hands. You do not use it for the church's utilities or even to pay for his hotel room. If the church decides to add more to the honorarium, so be it; but ethics requires that you keep your word.

The method of receiving the tithes and offerings is a matter of taste and purpose. Some pass a collection receptacle; others have the people come forward to make their gifts; and others receive the tithe in permanent boxes placed conspicuously in the building and still receive offerings during the service as a specific act of worship. Style of method is a choice; reverential joy in practice is essential. As such, you should never let any gift or giver receive personal notice during any public service. Everything that can be done should be done to afford the joy of a personal response of thanksgiving, obedience, and pleasure as the church honors God and His Word during the acts of tithing and giving.

67. The Ethic of Dispersing Church Monies

The church represents the Lord, not only in worship and ministry, but also in ethical financial procedures. Every dollar must be accounted for. Every designated gift must be honored and used as such. If for any reason, you feel that the money received by the church violates the principles of Scripture, it should be returned to the donor. For example, on occasion I had offerings given and dedicated for a cause that would adversely affect the church; I had that gift returned with a proper explanation. If it was made anonymously, it was placed in the general fund to be used for some proper need.

Every bill should be paid in full or partial payment made preceded by a phone call of explanation. When starting a church, there may come a time (poor stewardship and/or planning) when there is not enough money to pay the pastor (a few times of this and things will tighten up spiritually); when this happens, the monthly (public) obligations must come first. In faith, I always saw that the bills were paid as they came in each month. Never have a church check sent out until every penny needed to cover it has already been deposited; I have in my time of ministry received a number of honorarium checks that bounced.

Please realize that this is really a felony.

One common mistake made by new churches when there is seemingly so little money is to maintain the church money and personal money in one account. Nothing can ruin more quickly the credibility of your ministry than this. Regardless of the paucity of funds, separate accounts. Individual accounting is a *must!*

68. Financial Records and Confidentiality

An individual's giving record kept by the church is a very personal thing and treated confidentially. The only people who have access to this information are the financial office workers that handle and record the giving information and the senior pastor of the church. Every office worker is by Christian ethics responsible to keep this information confidential.

However, the senior pastor of the church should be aware of each member's financial stewardship, just as he is responsible to know the status of other personal areas of each one in his flock. This may tend to put a heavy burden upon the pastor, being aware of such information. Even with the possibility of putting on him the pressure of bias that could affect his relationship with those members, as the shepherd of the flock he needs to know where each person in his flock is spiritually. This knowledge is so important for his prayers, teachings, and eventually counseling and advice, when called upon to do so.

69. Christian Ethics and Mammon

Honesty is the only policy for the church. Honesty is an ethic to be followed at all times. The Bible has much to say about this matter, but the standard of business in our society is hardly Christian; it is little more than pagan in ethic. Jesus commanded believers to be honest, even at the expense of a loss. The reputation of the Father in the earth is the church's responsibility.

Honesty is not limited to just paying your bills in full and on time; it is much more intricate than this. It includes how you pay your employees, how you guard yourself from plagiarizing, how you care for "widows indeed" (1 Timothy 5:1ff), how you do not take your Christian brother to civil court, how accurately and compassionately you tend to your responsibility of benevolence, and how you restrain from hype and exaggeration from the pulpit to the newspaper. These are just a few considerations of the honesty the church is responsible to perform with a WWJD format.

I believe that the local church is deeply responsible for not only its beginning (church planting, and I do believe in this), but also its posterity. Not only should we pay the preacher well, but also, what about the other fivefold ministries connected to or sent out from the church? I believe that we should provide for them as well. When this part of our church heritage is in need of medical and burial assistance, we should be delighted to help. If we don't, then who will be responsible?

An old traveling Bible teacher who came by our church annually to share his anointed insight of the Scriptures got sick and was near death. He and his dear wife lived in a tiny motor home and were several states away when we received word of his condition. As pastor, I felt obligated to call his spouse and check on his well-being and their financial status. He was dying, and they were broke. Our church family helped pay for his medical then burial expenses and went on to assist his widow on a monthly basis. Pastor, if your budget is so tight or lagging behind that you cannot respond to needs of true ministry that has served your church well, you may be following Cain's ethic, "Am I my brother's keeper?" rather than Jesus' ethic of *honesty.*

Let me mention another trap of *mammon:* building buildings beyond the necessary comfort of the people and putting up a palace, with missions having no real place in your budget; or you believe that your TV ministry takes the place of the Great Commission of Jesus, and you are not honest in your financial obligations according to Scripture.

This is how the church should handle its material possessions: being accountable, responsible, caring, sharing, and always serving God but never serving mammon. These are the criteria of Christian honesty.

70. How to Teach Stewardship in Your Church

According to Scripture, pastors are "apt to teach." Preaching comes from the Spirit via the heart (emotions) and, as purposed, causes an immediate response within hearers; teaching comes from the Spirit via the mind and usually has a permanent effect upon its hearers. That is why your math teacher did not preach: ***"Two** . . . hallejuah! **plus two** . . . glory to God! **equals four** . . . praise His Name for ever!"* No, he taught you two plus two equals four, and you have remembered it to this day!

You can never stop teaching on a subject until it is being practiced in people's daily lives. Financial stewardship is so imperative and fundamental to victorious Christian living and serving that it is to our negligence and the detriment of others that we do not teach, with the emphasis on rote, its basic understanding.

Many pastors have a misperception about teaching about money. The devil tells them that they will be perceived as panhandlers. This is a lie! Years ago I was asked to speak in both morning services at a church, and when I got there, the pastor asked me (as a teacher) to teach on tithing. No problem. I asked him when he had last spoken on the subject, and he let me know that in more than five years, he had never given one sermon on the subject. A while after I arrived home, he sent word that his offerings had gone up $5,000 per week, and he gave that one message the credit.

People will do what they are *taught* to do. Ignorance, not rebellion, is the chief culprit for causing a church's weak financial base. Also, you mustn't fail to mention the personal blessings that come as a result of the tither's obedience.

I always prepared an annual series on financial stewardship for my church. A series (four to six messages) is necessary to drive home a set of truths pertaining to personal Christian stewardship. You know that people are not going to tithe consistently if they do not have their act together with their personal finances. They need to be taught the disciplines of earning money, spending money, saving money, investing money, and giving money. People must learn the true priority of financial management; with the Christian it starts with the tithe, that is, God comes *first!*

Of course, you realize that I am not propounding a hyper-prosperity syndrome, but negligence in your financial responsibility to your people is hyper-wrong! Any teaching, or the lack of it, that is not kept in balance with the whole of Christian doctrine becomes by itself *heresy.*

71. How to Set Precedents and Make Church Policies

One of the things that you as pastor must learn is that every time you make a decision (grant permission, start something), you are setting a *precedent* for your present ministry. If you allow something, even the most trivial thing, to begin, you are really breaking ground for what will become in the eyes of the people an established order. If you do it for one, you must do it for all—no exceptions—unless you want to cause an emotional war to be declared and carried on. Talk about the traditional opening of a can of worms—this is it!

People will ask a favor, make a suggestion (to them it is the brainstorm of the year), or ask you to pass judgment in a certain area when you are the least prepared to make a competent decision, like when you have just finished preaching or are going to an important meeting with much on your mind. I learned early in my ministry to always, initially say, "We'll see." This will postpone your decision until you have had serious time to consider it, and this will do it in a very congenial way. In good time, after prayer and careful evaluation of the total ramifications concealed in this apparently innocent request, you will be able to handle the request so it will be the best decision for all the church all the time. Most of the time these requests or ideas that are given are intensely personal and/or deviate from normal practice and have no precedent that has been previously established.

The correct way to escape from this continual pressure is to establish church policies that will impersonally guide daily church life. These policies will remove you and others from personal involvement in decisions that could normally disrupt or antagonize church family relationships. Church policies fall into several categories: staff relationships, office relationships, and general social relationships. Before analyzing each category, you need to see how natural this system becomes. When you are asked to add, change, or grant a favor, you will need time to see how this decision is going to affect the general congregation long-term.

Let's present a situation that frequently comes up. A member of the church requests to use the church kitchen and fellowship facilities to host his parents' fiftieth wedding anniversary. The simple facts are they are good members of the church and fiftieth wedding anniversaries are always to be lauded. Again, there will be only two dozen people involved, and they promise to restore the area to its state of readiness before Sunday church services.

Once you grant this permission, you are writing a precedent "in stone." Soon, you can be certain, someone just as qualified will want to celebrate their fourth wedding anniversary, using the church's facilities. You can count on it, someone will like the "family" idea and want to hold his grandchild's birthday party there; then comes a graduation reception, a new job celebration, Thanksgiving dinner, and someone will want to use the church facility for a twentieth high school class reunion. The list will never end. The facilities will be left unclean. There will be arguments over calendar discrepancies, and the *war* goes on.

What needs to be done is to write a policy that is fair to the purpose of the church facilities and takes into consideration a nondiscriminatory plan for all members of the fellowship. Now you will not have to explain all the problems that this request has caused in the past. You will not have to come across as a dictator or an unloving person. You will not be caught off guard to make an impromptu decision that has not been prayed about and studied out. You simply defer the matter to an *impersonal* policy that the church is obligated to follow. It is that easy.

As stated earlier, you will find several areas in which policies will serve you well. One of these areas is within your staff. This is because the staff will generally have distinctive relationships that can grant certain privileges to highly responsible persons, keeping in mind that fairness is necessary among staff members. Such things as length of vacation, days off, and certain other privileges, as well as their families' involvement in the ministry, should be clearly spelled out to staff members.

Office policies are helpful in the areas of dress, break

times, bringing children (nursing mothers) to work, etc., and will stop any number of problems without having to inject what could be construed at the time as personal favoritism or unfairness.

Policies that define the general social life (many scenarios have no direct scriptural teaching) within the church family will really help. These policies are usually written from hindsight, so don't go through a difficult time twice. Written policies ensure that hard decisions that usually carry with them lasting effects are dealt with quietly and impersonally. Again, these policies need not be included in your new member orientation or approved in any public way. Policies amount to an executive directive that is written down, alleviating personality conflicts and precluding any appearance of prejudice.

72. How to Make Your Pulpit Ministry Effective

There are four challenges to making your preaching ministry effective. The first of the four is *to know God's "heart word" for the hour.* Not serving "stale bread" has little to do with repeating a successful message as the Spirit brings it up; it is not the sermon that needs to be fresh, but the quickened word God has laid upon your heart as the pressing need of the hour. Only God can successfully quicken your spirit to the challenge of the hour—not circumstances or emotional needs (as real as they may be). As you ponder the Word of God, the Spirit is already highlighting the thought of the hour, and without fail the two will unite and spawn a "God word" to your heart. The Spirit can direct you to your next message as you pray and meditate; however, you must hear from heaven, not from the television or newspaper and much less from someone else's passion.

The second thing that will ensure a message from God that He desires to enforce upon His people through their undershepherd is *proper* preparation. Notice that I did not say *adequate* preparation; preparation is not intended for you to feel good about yourself (if it does, you have missed your purpose). Proper preparation means that you study until you will be preaching from the overflow. If you only get filled with the message, all you have is what is in it for you. You are only warming up a TV dinner for one. Stay with your study and stay in the presence of God until you are like a glass under a faucet that has failed to turn off. (I always have an hour more to say than what God wants the congregation to hear for any one sermon.) Preach from the overflow.

The third thing that is essential to an effective message is praying over the message and the coming occasion until you itch with excitement over the opportunity. Prayer causes the release of purpose, motivation, and clarity that causes the power to accomplish God's intended purpose for that hour. Remember: Jesus prayed through His experience on the cross at Gethsemane and never wavered one degree through the total ordeal of crucifixion. This same clarity and power gained through prayer will bring purpose and anticipation to sharing God's Word for that moment to your people.

The fourth thing that will afford a successful pulpit experience is your meditation. The last contact you have before entering the pulpit should be with God's Spirit. Every athletic team listens intently to the last words of the coach as they run out to the field of play; so ought God's pastors. His presence and counsel and His affirmation of you and the message, along with the anointing, are crucial for His success through you.

When troops are on the front line of a battle waiting

for the signal to attack, every ear is poised to hear the leading officer's command. When it comes, there is no time for distractions, small talk, or further considerations. Just follow your orders and do your best, with a heart full of loyalty to Him and purpose for the hour.

Preaching is fun, but if it is just fun, it is selfish. However gifted the trumpet player may be, playing without music is nothing more than confusing nonsense and noise. We must be fully dedicated to the preaching of His Word for the hour to our people.

73. Grasping the Main Purpose of the Church

For centuries the purpose of the church has been misunderstood at best and just plain missed for the most part. Understandably, one of the main functions of the church is the sanctification of the believer; another purpose is the discovery and implementation of gifts and ministries within the believer. Oftentimes social and civil responsibilities have been either absent or excessive within congregations.

It is exceptional to find a congregation and its leaders seriously undertaking the main purpose of the church: the winning of the world to Christ. Jesus had a "world facing eternity" consciousness, as seen by His last command in the Gospels and in the book of Acts. The reason the church has forfeited His commission is that, for the most part, it has not understood why He gave such a commission in the first place.

God is a God of love. Man, His final creation (not nature or animals, though I appreciate people's appreciation of nature), was made for the sole purpose of having a loving relationship with Him. The Scriptures tell us that God intended for myriads of men to ultimately be worshipping Him (see the crescendo of multitudes mentioned at the end times in the book of Revelation).

In the beginning, God created only Adam and Eve and told them to begin working on His plan, and He gave them the principle of multiplication. Multiplication works. Jesus chose twelve men and commissioned them to bring the world to Him through the principle of multiplication, and the early church started by "adding" believers; they soon moved into the principle of multiplication, as we note in the book of Acts.

Churches today are content with the principle of addition. Many churches have very few additions each year. They apparently have missed the major purpose of God for eternity: millions upon millions of redeemed members of mankind filling a new heaven and a new earth and all worshipping and loving Him.

If each one will begin by winning one soul and then accept the responsibility of mentoring twelve people by teaching them to do the same, the church will automatically enter the principle of multiplication. One wins twelve. The 12 each win 12, which equals 144. The 144 each win 12, equaling 1,728. The 1,728 each win and mentor 12, which now equals 20,736 souls; thus, in four generations your church would have more than 20,000 members.

Will it work? As pastor, you preach and expect all your members to be holy, to tithe, and to read their Bibles. Why not expect them to perform God's greatest purpose, bringing souls to Him? They will, if you will lead the way and teach them to do so.

74. How to Stand in Truth

We have been commissioned to minister the truth. However, we must realize that at best we have only a part of the truth. There is a story of three blind men who visited the petting zoo. They were allowed to touch an elephant, and as they discussed it among themselves, they fell into an argument as to what an elephant was like. One felt the trunk and became certain that an elephant was like a tree. The second man placed his hands on the elephant's side, and he contended that an elephant was just like a wall. The third blind man, having touched the elephant's tail, was sure that the elephant was nothing more than a rope. Two thoughts: (1) what you perceive is truth to you and (2) the truth you *have* is only partial. We all may have several pieces of the puzzle, but we do not have all the *pieces.*

Truth is more than philosophical; philosophy is the search for truth, as Pontius Pilate spoke. Again, truth is narrow, not like literature, but rather like math: two plus two equals four. Truth is not relative. Feelings or emotions do not give forth truth. Truth is not rational; it is not figured out in your mind: it is! Truth is self-evident. I can be wrong about it and change, or I can be ignorant about it and learn; but it is there! Truth is its own standard; no one measures a yardstick before using it. Finally, truth is the parameter of and the basis for unity.

We will (can) only come into true unity based upon our mutual understanding of truth. This is why unity, though much talked about, is so sparse within our ranks. It becomes our responsibility in seeking unity to start where we agree on truth and not start fussing about our differences. Men can only agree to disagree about their differences, and that is not unity; so let's not allow our differences to destroy our common understanding of truth (however limited), and let's have at least that much unity. If an article in the store costs $1 and I have only 85 cents, I do not throw the 85 cents away because I don't have the required dollar. I wait and save up the needed 15 cents and *then* go and purchase the needed item.

75. How to Handle People Leaving Your Church

People will leave your church eventually, and it is wise to know why they leave and how you, their shepherd, should handle their leaving. It is inevitable that people in our culture will change jobs or need to move when they are out of a job, and really there are a number of good reasons why some people will leave your church.

On the other hand, there are numerous situations when people decide to leave your church, but for the wrong reasons. Some (weaker ones) are victimized by proselytizing. Some people lose sight of the vision of the house, or they begin to develop a different vision. This always results in their becoming disenchanted. On occasion, there are those people who change their polarity doctrinally, and when that happens, if they cannot receive correction, they need to leave.

Other people have not matured sufficiently to know the difference between friendship and fellowship. They may come into the church led by another member, and when that member gets mad and leaves, they do also—relationship built on friendship. Christians must realize that they are in fellowship with Jesus and not allow personal friendships to intervene with their fellowship with Jesus. Some members have not placed themselves under the spiritual authority of the church and become offended or rebellious when they are challenged or corrected. Some believers need affirmation and a place to serve, and when they are overlooked, they lose hope and ultimately leave your church. The greatest reason for people to leave a church is that they have accepted an offense. Until this is recognized and dealt with, they will leave the church or cause others to leave.

How you respond to this leaving will make a big difference in your ministry, their lives, and the lives of those still in the church. If people must leave for legitimate reasons, you should pray with them personally, bless them publicly, and when necessary, help them to relocate to a new church home. When you have those who leave wrongly, your reaction is critical. If they are angry, you stay calm. If they are in rebellion or sin, you clarify the issue, remembering that God did not get Moses to dig Korah's hole. Always be prepared to go the second mile with them, and know that there are no "no reasons."

Learn how to cope with this scenario of leaving. Do not get into rejection over it; this is not the ultimate failure in ministry. Do not allow any "soul ties" to remain that will hinder both you and them. Remember that all the days and lessons they spent with you were "learning" days in their lives. Hopefully, you will be able to send them off, just as you would marry off your daughter; and if not, just be quietly relieved and exclaim, "Whew!"

76. Grasping the Ministry's Ultimate Responsibility

In the book of Numbers, God explains the ultimate function of ministry (Chapter 1:47–54). It helps to see the presence of fivefold ministry (typical): Moses, Aaron, the Kohathites, the Gershonites, and the Merarithites placed around the tabernacle of God. The ministry was placed there for two reasons: The first reason was to keep the people from deliberately or ignorantly infringing on God's holiness, becoming too familiar with God and losing reverence and thus a loss of relationship. The second reason for the ministry being between God and the people was to grant assistance to the people in their daily lives and their service to God (the function of the priesthood in the role of mediator).

If the people came in an unauthorized way before God, the reaction was like the focus of your eye: the object becomes blurred if too close or too far away. Signs of this unauthorized coming to God today by the church are the nonchalance over personal sin and attempting to come into the presence of God or coming to the promises of God in unbelief. Again, overfamiliarity on the people's part is a wrong approach to God and must be challenged and changed by ministry.

Again, your responsibility as a minister is to assist your people in their pursuit of and service to Jesus. As a priest (mediator and leader), you are to lead them correctly in the worship of God. As a minister, you are responsible that they hear from God correctly and continually. To do this requires that your witness be truly an exemplary lifestyle.

77. Five Faults Found in Leaders

These five problem areas are either in excess or lack within the life of the minister of the Lord. One of the leading weaknesses in ministry today is the fluent use of hype. I call hype the intentional excess of verbiage verging on deception. It is glorifying the "unhappened," confusing the sensual with the spiritual, and giving a wrong priority to a thing on the list of important things. Finally, I call it the creation of the "popular." Never once is there any hint of hype in the ministry expressions of the New Testament. If something is important to God, it is important with or without stereo or three-dimensional presentation. The opposite error to hype found in ministry is to harbor rejection. Rejection is evaluating your acceptance wrongly, the fruit of a torn ego.

Another fault found in ministry is the stewardship of time, the unwillingness to live with a schedule that is properly prioritized. Your *ministry* is not above the time needed for prayer, a good relationship with your family, and giving or delegating adequate time to the people of your church. You are not the Holy Spirit, and time and your choice on how to use it are fallible at best. On the other hand, laziness is a self- imposed disregard for God's most important gift to you in this world outside of salvation:

time. When you disregard effective and efficient use of your time, it creates a waste that is impossible to correct or retrieve. Laziness is the fruit of a very poor work ethic, the flip side of being driven.

A third fault found within ministry is the narrow and sole dependence upon organization. Order is a chief evidence of Holy Spirit control in one's life, but to organize anything without the life of the Spirit and His control is the same as marrying a mannequin: you have form, but no life. On the other hand, you are in trouble if you lack vision. A person without vision is the same as someone who attempts to drive a car while it is in neutral: there is lots of noise, but no motion. Every car needs a windshield and every ministry needs vision, which is God's plan and expectation for your life work. If you spend your days attending to each thing that comes up in your daily life, you will never have time for, nor will you notice, that there is no forward motion in your life; your days will be wasted on secondhand priorities, and in the ministry they are nonending.

The fourth fault found within the ministry occurs when it becomes too political. Let me define the word *political* as practiced by ministry. To be politically correct is to conform to the opinions held by the loudest voice or the largest giver in the church, or to follow the route of least resistance. It is easily identified by such concepts as *convenience, compromise,* and vague *convictions.* It leaves you as the pastor with the sense of being just a hireling or "yes man." To the other extreme is the use of doctrine in a political sense, which is just another way of describing *heresy.* Heresy is the extension of one doctrinal truth beyond and out of balance of all other doctrines. When the doctrine of faith or healing or prosperity or tongues, to name a few, becomes grossly disproportionate to other doctrinal tenets, it becomes heretical. Balance is the needed practice for "rightly dividing the word of truth."

The last fault to mention is related to a default in our culture: conducting your ministry professionally. Professionalism in the church is having a high standard of *charisma* and expertise that is devoid of God's spirit of compassion. On the other hand, many ministries practice *commercialism* that is nothing more than a Wall Street mentality and practice that have been whitewashed in consumer euphemisms (e.g., you don't *sell* stuff, rather, "you *need* our product, and it can be yours for an *offering* that is not less than $——; so call *now!*"). I believe you get my point.

78. How to Have Order in Your Life

Spiritual government is made up of three entities: spiritual authority, order, and divine wisdom. Let us focus on the establishment of *order.* Order must be present in three areas of your personal life before it ever can be accomplished in your ministry: (1) Your time must be spent in an orderly manner. (2) Your relationships must be in order. (3) Your possessions must be maintained in godly order. From the beginning when the Spirit of God comes in, He changes chaos into divine order (Genesis 1:2).

Disorder is the word placed on a sign that signifies that something is broken. Most people suffer with a lot of "broken" stuff. Many attempt to live lives that are very much like a lady's purse (bag). It's all there, I suppose; all you need is a metal detector and several spare batteries to find it!

You must have order within your time, or your schedule. That means no missed appointments. Your devotional life happens as much as you love the Lord; if this is the case, many believers have no time for God! It is just as easy to set your clock thirty minutes fast so you can be on time, that is, until your Christian conviction of tardiness catches up with you. Don't spend excessive time doing what you are not good at. Work always has a sense of punctuality, whereas play has little to no understanding for time. Appointments, due dates, and promises are based upon honest treatment of time, all of which have a great deal to say about your Christian integrity.

There must be divine order present in your life's relationships to permit bonding and affirmation and to allow for love to be effectively communicated. Your relationship with the Father, Son, and Holy Spirit must become your first dedication and love. Your wife and children come next, and then the rest in the pecking order are to be given the time required for proper devotion, care, and covering. Your work must take its place right after your responsibilities to your nation, and all the rest can "pick over the bones."

Possessions must be kept in order to eliminate confusion, poor discipline, and shoddy stewardship. You don't want to have a vehicle that looks like a landfill on wheels. Your front yard is a picture of your outward application of order, and your clothes closet is a good replica of your inner man.

Order, like cleanliness, is godly, and like winding a clock, it is something you must do to allow it to operate. Like everything else, it will become second nature to you as you practice it.

79. How to Eliminate Poor Communication

As a minister, one of your prime responsibilities is to *communicate* successfully, not only from the pulpit, but also in every place and with each person who crosses your path. Many have difficulties with this and may not understand their problem. Go through this checklist and evaluate your skills that may directly affect this important part of your life's ministry.

Poor communication begins with unspoken thoughts. These unspoken thoughts leave the other person with only a partial, hazy understanding. Semantics (word definition) is the reason that many arguments continue—all because of a different definition of one little word. Imagine the frustration of having a cabinet filled with wrongly labeled cans.

Preconceived ideas (prejudice) assumed about a person or situation do mayhem to communication. So does speaking the truth, but not speaking it in love. Discretion and tact go a long way in having good communication (e.g., A boy looks into the eyes of an ugly girl and says, "When I look into your eyes, time stands still," instead of saying, "Your face would stop an eight-day clock.") Surgeons use anesthesia, not for their sakes, but for their patients.

Feelings of inadequacy have the same effect in

communication as does a bridge being out on a road. Again, have sufficient facts about what you are discussing, or listen and learn. Half of communication is talking, and the other half is *listening.* Learn to be a good listener. To be a good listener takes maturity, love, and a lot of patience.

Spiritual preparedness is essential for productive communication. Such things as preferring your brother, adequate prayer, and understanding your delegated authority are all necessary for successful communication.

Watch your words. They should never be *adulterated,* saying words with feeling but to the wrong person (wrong motive). Words should not be *qualified,* saying some words but not all the words (equal to a half-truth). Insincerity and selfish motives all but destroy communication.

One last area in communication is your body language. You speak not only with your mouth, but also with your gestures, facial expressions, and body movements. For good communication, prepare to do so with the total you! Your excitement, rapport, and interest promoted by body language will make a huge difference in your communication.

80. How to Have a Growing Church

For anything to grow, it must be and stay alive. Recently a comprehensive survey was made by Christian A. Schwarz that shows seven distinctive factors of *growing* churches around the world. The growth should have both qualitative and quantitative goals: (1) They lead people to use their giftings and leadership. (2) They have a passionate spirituality. (3) They have functional structures that can grow past traditional modes and methods. (4) There is inspiring worship. (5) There are small groups that are alive and that multiply. (6) There is evangelism that meets the needs of spirit, soul, and body. (7) There are full and loving relationships. It should be noted that the survey found that No. 5 (small groups that are alive and multiply) was the No. 1 prerequisite to inspire and sustain growth in all the churches surveyed.

The principle of twelve ordained by Jesus as He chose, mentored, and commissioned His twelve apostles is the plan of God that Jesus demonstrated and commanded us to use to fill the earth with disciples. As noted in Genesis 1, God provided for, commanded, and expected Adam and Eve to multiply. Jesus commissioned His church to go into all the world and make disciples. The book of Revelation repeatedly refers to the myriad of multitudes before God's throne in eternity. In the book of Acts, the early church picked up momentum and moved from "adding daily to the church" to "multiplying." Until recently, the church for the last two thousand years has failed to grasp God's plan for church growth: multiplication.

Jesus equipped and then expected his twelve apostles to multiply, which happened. Churches were planted in all the known world within one hundred years of the resurrection of Jesus. So it can and should be with the churches today. The plan is ultrasimple: One person (the pastor) selects twelve men who grasp this vision of evangelism through multiplication and prepares them with seven easy lessons to participate in an Encounter (a three-day retreat that has men encounter the cross of Jesus, resulting in a two-year spiritual advance in sanctification in each participant). Immediately the pastor disciples them or reviews with them in ten lessons the basics of Christian responsibility, as they are now attending, being challenged, and edified in his weekly group meeting. The pastor now leads them into three twelve-week terms of leadership training. Now they, too, can begin their own cells and begin to win twelve others to the Lord and so *repeat* the process.

When the pastor has twelve men who follow his lead to win and see discipled their own twelve men (this will take a couple of years), this one man (the pastor) now has 144 men attending weekly group meetings and being trained. When the 144 follow the process, you soon have 1,728 in living cells. When these repeat the process (multiply), the church will have 20,736 members in four short generations (about six years) after beginning the Lord's plan for *multiplication.*

The success of this fruitfulness is found in the spirit of evangelism raging in fever pitch in his people, along with a long track of discipleship that solidifies the new converts and keeps them from backsliding. Statistics show that in less than two years, your church will go from an 80 percent loss of new members to an amazingly low 20 percent going out the "back door" of your church. If you are interested to learn more about this, you are free to contact me by e-mail at jlclark3@cox.net.

81. Four Aspects of Healthy Sheep

As the undershepherd, you can have the joyful experience of watching your sheep become and stay healthy and productive. The first thing you can provide is for them to feel safe in God's house. You do this by letting them feel encouraged without condemnation. They are free to become and to do their best by being able to express themselves without pressure. Threats of coercion or feelings of being used never arise in their hearts, and they know that you have their best interests at heart in every area of their lives. They can feel secure in your doctrinal integrity and your purity of heart and motive, and they know that you are always *for them,* even if they should do something wrong.

Another thing you can provide is the knowing that they are and feel pastored. Many just attend church, sometimes all their lives, but never get to feel pastored. Others come to your services simply because they like your preaching. Your goal should be to become the pastor to every legitimate member. It is the Holy Spirit that provides opportunities for this relationship to form. You can pray that the Spirit opens the door for this opportunity to take place so that at least one member in each family will know you are their pastor. This relationship may be deferred until some trauma happens to the family: death, sickness, financial adversity, or some happy time such as a birth, a wedding, or a graduation. You must stand ready and be sensitive for this time to arrive, and you must be quick in the Spirit to capitalize on the open door to serve your sheep and earn the relationship as pastor.

A third thing you can do is to encourage your sheep to take ownership of *their* church. They know that it is Jesus who invited them to become a part of this church, and it is the Holy Spirit that continually sponsors their acceptance in their church. They can also feel vitally connected as they continue in covenant relationship with the local body through the Lord's Supper, congregational worship, leading in prayer, and helping with the invitation. Becoming a part of a vital small group meeting will also enlarge the sense of ownership as they watch new converts come in under their watch.

Fourthly, the sense of ownership comes as they join in with ministering. The gifts of the Spirit allow each one to have a part in a service. Testimonies are a valid way to not only support the church but to also encourage others to grow in their faith. Then, of course, there is their responsibility and opportunity to give, both in tithes and offerings. Ownership is also encouraged as they give of their time and talents to service opportunities and through short-term missions trips.

A healthy sheep is one that has the assurance and acceptance that happens when thoroughly connected.

This realization will come not only through the pastor, but also through the sheep themselves as they foster this confidence to one another as relationships are formed.

82. How Accountability Helps

It is a known fact that being in the ministry draws Satan's attacks to you like flies to honey. However, there are as many men who fail in the ministry because of their own undoing from within as there are those that succumb to the devil's relentless attacks from without. Men in the ministry have a way of setting up their own booby traps. Before I mention a few, let me admonish you to put in place the most positive and successful way to overcome a ministerial blowout: become and remain *accountable.*

This does not mean being accountable just to an organization or a letterhead overseer, or as many proclaim, "I answer just to God." Each minister needs to be actively and personally accountable. Make it someone who will ask you, "What are *you* doing?" Better yet, have such an intimate relationship with him that you become convicted if you don't report unto him. I know this does not placate the flesh, but it certainly helps to keep your motivation straight and your ethics pure.

The booby trap of sex is a dangerous instrument. You must endeavor to keep your mind clean and pure of improper motives. This will help control your mouth so that you will not use suggestive terms or terms of endearment with the opposite sex, in any circumstance. You must keep your hands from any touch that could possibly be construed as a sexual advance. Employ the "six-inch rule" with people of the opposite sex. Never allow yourself to be placed in (or for that matter make one yourself) a compromising position, such as being alone in a room with someone of the opposite sex or going to her residence when she is home alone. Never have a meal with a woman with just the two of you present, no matter how trivial or important the meeting may be.

The booby trap of money is almost as scandalous and just as dangerous. You desperately need accountability for every cent of ministry money within your responsibility. This includes proper accounting for petty cash and any charges made to or by the ministry. Make certain every receipt is correct and properly and promptly turned in. The misappropriation of offerings and donations, using them for purposes other than their designated ones, is scandalous. I never would allow myself to privately take someone else's cash offering or tithe to the church; I asked the person to defer his giving until he was privileged to bring it himself. You are to abstain from every appearance of evil. What might appear to be an innocent request or gesture can turn sour; your ministerial witness is more valuable than seeming, for the moment, unkind.

Finally, the booby trap of ministry itself can blow your highest aspirations and purposes to pieces if you are not completely, continually accountable. You cannot justify any possibility of a compromise just because you can call it "ministry" (e.g., a wrong counseling relationship). You need not ever allow your person or reputation to be thought of or spoken of as greater than it *really* is; that is pride. Watch out for a messianic complex that can cause you to grow isolated or to use people as pawns to further your ministry. A number of so-called large ministries have tried climbing the corporate ladder, but usually in the wake of many hurt and ruined lives that were fired or discarded as they advanced themselves; they are answerable to God.

Stay accountable. If you are not accountable, become accountable! You, like everyone else, know at least one person who loves you, has confidence in your ministry, and will stick by your side no matter what, but who at the same time, will nail you at the slightest sign of a misdemeanor. That person is a friend worth his weight in gold.

83. Do Not Misjudge Your Ministry

Do not misjudge the effectiveness of your communication. Most pastors make the mistake of thinking their responsibility ends with their sermonizing. Your ability to preach may not be the same as the content of your preaching. Most church members (90 percent) do not know or understand your vision because they have never (rarely) heard it. This is why teaching is so necessary for the church: to get the facts presented with rote. Very few have a wide enough interest to cause them to remember something they heard just one time.

Do not misjudge the grace given you for ministry. There is a wrong idea that states that the longer you live and serve in the ministry, the easier it becomes. Nonsense! The apostle Paul was not the last one to hear these words from the Lord: "My grace is sufficient." The longer you serve, the harder it becomes; but His grace continually exceeds any difficulty you might have in serving Him.

Do not misjudge the anointing. Most of us pray frantically to see it flow out upon our ministries and then won't live there. Anointing works like a spotlight: it is on, but you have to stay where it is.

Do not misjudge your carnal nature. It never becomes holy. Success does not change it—only crucifixion. Like a spoiled child, it is going to "show out," but you never know when or where.

Do not misjudge your worth. Some have the idea that the longer they are in the ministry, the more they deserve, such as money, recognition, and attention. This is immature and childish; Jesus closed His earthly ministry by washing the feet of the very ones who should have shown Him honor but who wound up forsaking Him.

Do not misjudge your weaknesses. Except for a few persons, probably your greatest weakness is not having an abiding sense of confidence and regularly getting pulverized by rejection. This thwarts your ability to be transparent, stopping you from building strong relationships and delaying your improvement by your never being able to receive constructive criticism.

Do not misjudge your wounds. Hurts are a constant hazard of ministry, and if you don't get healed by releasing forgiveness, they will become an "infected" *offense.* You must be instant with repentance and forgiveness.

Do not misjudge your office. Your office comes inherent with delegated authority. Therefore, you must stay *others' conscious* to keep from abusing it. Remember: Authority is like your health; you never realize how great it is until you lose or misuse it. There should be those who are *ahead* of you in the ministry as well as many *behind* you. If this is not the case, you are not operating in an office; you are just playing a game.

84. Why You Can't Quit

Romans 11:28 reminds us that the callings of God cannot be eliminated or terminated—a harsh word for Monday mornings when our flesh is ready to quit again. Those in the ministry may say this with tongue in cheek, yet the virus of discouragement is a common ailment. The denominational world reports that it is losing ministers every week, and some groups are experiencing an acute shortage of trained and ordained ministers.

Pastors normally fall into one of three groups of "pro-quitters": (1) First is the pastor who is sheep-sensitive; he is people-oriented. His problem is that in time he faces losing 80 percent of his people (average for a program-based church)—enough to make anyone feel like quitting. (2) Second is the pastor who is administratively minded; this guy is project-oriented. His discouragement comes from a never-ending lack of money, time, or qualified people to volunteer with the vision. (3) The third type of pastor is pulpit-minded; he is gift-centered. He is a darling in the pulpit, but a loner and an "odd bird" out (relationally). If he could do anything else (auto mechanic, draftsman, etc.) but still have a pulpit, he would quit.

But no matter how great the lack or how unresolved the problems may be, you are under a mandate from God, and quitting is absolutely out of the question. And even if you do quit and do something else, you are still answerable to God for the indelible call upon your life. There is just no quitting!

Ministry is not about success or the lack of it; it is all about your call. When God planned the earth, your call was included. You must have and keep this eternal perspective about ministry (Paul warns us to judge ourselves regularly), and you must measure your ministry from God's perspective. Being called from the womb (Galatians 1:15), you have a lifetime obligation (Romans 11:29); even if you quit, you are still liable. And if you fail, you are destined to be restored.

Your call is like manna, that is, your source of strength is provided daily, along with your supply of vision. Feelings, needs, and hurts are just bumps in the road.

Your call supersedes your giftings. God gave you the giftings you need to complete your responsibility; it is up to you to discover them and use them in stewardship. You will find what you enjoy doing for God is what He has planned for you to do; just put away all the other distractions. Remember: Your call is not a competitive sport. You don't play to win; you are a winner *called* to play!

85. Fathers Make Us Accountable

The first and only problem Father God ever had was the defection and rebellion of Lucifer. This is the precedent He has set for all rebellion. To keep us from rebellion and ultimate failure, God has set "fathers" in the church.

Every son should be in a viable relationship with a father. Fatherhood goes beyond *siring* and requires a stable and ongoing relationship. Despite this spiritual principle, there is a fatherless syndrome within much of the ministry today that is caused by the lack and fear of accountability. The results are devastating. There are several signs that diagnose the problem: (1) Isolationism—caused by rejection and feelings of inferiority that naturally cause you to isolate yourself. (2) Busyness—the minister's security blanket. Busyness is a cover-up for having no real peace or direction in your ministry. (3) Self-importance—ministry that is 10 percent God-led and 90 percent self-driven. Just look at your personal devotional life. (4) Hypocrisy—expecting your people to be submitted and accountable while you are not.

Take this self-test and check yourself for your accountability: (1) You have difficulty determining the difference between the *good* and the *best.* (2) You evade church discipline and consequently stay in conflict with those members who seemingly won't submit. (3) You have not communicated effectively the vision of the house. (4) You have a problem handling correction.

Every minister needs a father relationship in his life and ministry. It adds balance, wisdom, confidence, and peace for each day and in every decision. When you walk with a father, you will find yourself walking also with brother ministers. A father can guide and help keep you focused in your vision. Most of all, only a father will afford that much needed affirmation and acceptance that so quickly bleeds away each time you face conflict.

86. How to Get Results from Fasting

Most pastors realize that fasting (voluntary abstinence from anything) does not in any way coerce God to do anything but will, in fact, help them to draw closer to Him and to better know His will. Jesus' teaching in the Gospels clearly shows us that this practice is solely extolled by grace and that He placed no rigid, religious rules upon it. While fasting, hunger pains are designated signals to remind us of our goal in praying.

However, Isaiah 58 offers some candid insight into fasting. Isaiah declares several things that will absolutely nullify any attempt to fast. Complaining during the time of fasting, complaining about the situation for which you are praying, and/or complaining about the physical and emotional discomfort caused by fasting will derail your prayer and fasting.

It is self-defeating to bring hype and drama to be a part of fasting, as did the prophets of Baal in Elijah's time. Jesus clearly says to downplay the rigors caused by fasting; making a public display of your fasting simply thwarts your purpose.

You cannot fast to help you better concentrate on God's will for a specific need while enjoying fleshly pleasures at the same time. To forgo food but to enjoy a movie or play golf is a direct conflict of interests. Paul even mentions abstaining from your conjugal rights during the time of prayer and fasting.

In all reality, you cannot pursue your normal labor or job and expect your seeking God to be honest or effective. Wisdom would decree that you plan your fast for a time when this time will be able to produce the planned and needed results; just like doing your regular workload while on vacation would be an obvious conflict of interests, so it is with fasting and doing your job.

Things that can assist prayer and fasting are having a generous perception about the poor and needy, courage to speak God's word in difficult situations, learning how to correctly honor the Sabbath, and being instant in season and out of season, speaking God's word (revelation) into the lives of others.

The blessings derived from fasting while praying are beneficial. You can receive spiritual light and receive physical health. You can walk having God's righteousness in front of you and His glory behind you, and you can come into a real freedom in the Spirit.

87. The Pastor's Family and Divine Order

In no other place does the ministry face more adamant opposition and even attack from the world as we seek to bring it to the cross of Christ than in the arena of the *family.* The sovereignty and the integrity God has set in the home fly in the face of our present-day culture and its humanistic philosophy. Only by our most sensitive obedience to the Spirit and the Word of God will we be able to turn the tide and win this ruthless war against the home.

It is past time that we forsake lip service to the clearly pronounced priority of God; your family comes before your ministry, without exception. If as much time were spent on the preparation of the home as is spent in preparation for ministry, the present condition of the average minister's home would not be in such a deplorable state, with 30 percent of charismatic, Full Gospel pastors being divorced.

Other aspects of your ministry can be under wraps for a while (prayer, stewardship, and daily devotion), but not your family. The old adage that the minister's home is like a fishbowl is still true. Your family relationships speak and teach your church people as clearly as does your pulpit ministry. Strained relations within your family can be contained only briefly. Like your children, your people pick up quickly how the relationship between you and your wife really is. Know, too, that your marital relationship colors your pulpit ministry, and it does so in bold strokes. I know I can tell by attending just two or three services just how things are going in the pastor's home. You cannot be effective in the pulpit any more than you can be effective in your private devotions when there is strife, resentment, or neglect between you and your wife.

Your ministry is predicated upon your family—not the other way around. Only when you are building a loving, devoted, and happy family do you have a proper foundation for your ministry. Your family must worship and pray together, eat together, play together, and share family vision together. Of course, your worship time is centered at your church, and your family prayer time should exceed just the blessing at meals. Speaking of meals, eating together at least one meal a day is essential; eating is spiritual and is a part of the covenant relationship in your family. Family fun time is not always easy to accomplish because of variance of age and individual likes, but quality fun time is essential, even when you have to do some of it as a partial group at times. Of course, the family must understand the vision of the house, but each one in the family is discovering what God has for him or her in life, and these need to be shared as a team effort. It is most important that each family member know and regard the other members' places that God has for them.

Just a comment here: The principle of twelve really has a place for every family member, with commonality to each family member, providing goals that can be measured.

Everything else in life should be placed on hold until your family is enjoying a life of peace, love, and respect in the Lord. Once the family is first in your life, everything else will become *first-rate.*

88. How to Have a Pastor and Wife Ministry

Every pastor is full of expectations of being God's minister and is usually enthusiastic about it. On the other hand, a pastor's wife faces the ministry with a wide range of opinions, everything from feeling like it's "*his* ministry" to being a "barefoot mama" to competing with her husband for the pulpit. Although pastors' wives vary in opinion about ministry, one thing is certain: they are at their husbands' sides and are very much a part of the ministry—like it or not, involved or not! Their giftings will vary. The size of the family and the wife's schedule must be considered. But, being one with her husband, they are, for certain, in the ministry together.

The one thing that most wives lack is not gifting, ability, or even opportunity. What they lack is *affirmation* of their office that will release them into whatever ministry they have and make it fruitful. Their affirmation is the transfer by touch and vocal commendation of their place in the ministry. Affirmation is a qualified "yes" emanating from spiritual authority that releases and decrees the place and the right to minister. Every son and every daughter needs affirmation; so does the novice in the ministry. Every son of every father needs serious affirmation upon his life, and so does every pastor, regardless of age, need a father's (apostolic) affirmation.

Pastor, telling your wife who she is and what she should be doing doesn't work; you have tried this for some time without success. Affirmation is the connection of the Holy Spirit between a mentor and the person he is mentoring, between every father and his children, and between the minister and his wife. It is the serious laying on of hands (formally) and pronouncing, decreeing, adjuring, instructing, and releasing the gifting and authority upon her that comes from your office as pastor and husband. It is apostolic in nature. It is prophetic in nature. It is God's reassuring "yes" to all He has placed within your wife. She has this by virtue of being your wife. As your wife, she has access to your money, your name, your possessions, and your ministry. But like many married women, she may wear the ring yet not often feel (romantically) very married.

Until the pastor realizes that he has been "walking with one leg" in the ministry and comes to realize he is married to a woman who is both a mother and a minister, and then repents and affirms her, nothing will change. It starts with the husband. It also ends with the husband. Affirmation is like bathing: it is effective only upon repeated performances. Just as you must express your love to your wife regularly, you must regularly express the Father's affirmation to her through you.

89. Ministry Is Generational

Can your son take your place as the pastor of the church? The question sometimes is asked with a negative twist or often thought of but ignored because of culture or theology. Is it God to do this? Could it be dangerous nepotism? Then, some pastors are having such a discouraging time that they seriously want to shield their sons from such a fate. Let's look at this scenario a little more closely.

Every man with a son models much of his gifting. The son certainly has (could have) his dad as his role model. The Old World culture expected and was usually rewarded with a son following in his father's vocation, with much the same skills and maybe even more. The financial world passes its hold on life to the next generation. Monarchies are required by culture to pass the baton of rulership to the next generation, without exception, so why not the ministry?

The pastor presents his son(s) to the Lord for His agenda. The pastor raises his children in the admonition and nurture of the Lord. The son adapts quickly to his father's vision of service to God. So why would not God have already called them from the beginning? Within the ranks of the International Network of Local Churches (our fellowship of local churches), a precedent is being set and becoming culturally acceptable of a father turning the church over to a son. In my family, we are approaching this glorious phenomenon of father to son, to the third generation. The solidarity, peace, and continuity of vision that are taking place are simply marvelous. Remember: This is a blessing of the Lord and not a manmade piece of religious legislation.

90. How to Prioritize Your Home Schedule

If your family has priority over ministry, then the sensible thing to do is to set up your home calendar first, realizing that you are required to work and work will take its normal time slot. But from there on, family time must be prioritized.

God ordained the Sabbath, but He does not schedule committee meetings. Wisdom and fairness in this matter will resolve any serious spiritual conflicts or just plain *religious* ideas.

Every child in the family deserves special time (with the parents) as well as family times together. Quality time is essential. You can take your daughter to the zoo and spend the whole afternoon with her, but if your mind is on the building program, she will not get the attention she needs and deserves. What is more, she will feel neglected, even though she is only three, just the same way you would feel if your wife enjoyed an apple during your lovemaking. Prayer and concerted effort will allow you to hammer out an equitable calendar for your family.

When it comes to the private times with your wife, time, as well as money, usually plays a big part in filling in a calendar. As for the finances, I resort to *100 Creative*

Dating Ideas, most of which require just a small investment and are great fun. This needs to have a regular, set time.

Time with your wife should be regular, with time and expenses given consideration. How much time can you afford? Time is like money: you probably do not have much, but that doesn't stop you from "affording" it. I have devised a great compromise: my wife and I regularly take what we call a *minimoon*. We get away for two or three days alone at some bed and breakfast (anywhere, really). When a vacation is needed but time and money is limited, the minimoon does wonders. It can be as inexpensive as you want (provided you don't go shopping!).

The main thing is building and maintaining relationships within the family. The joy of personal attention is as rewarding as it is essential; just think of the blessings flowing from a *personal* time with the Lord.

91. How to Discipline Your Children

Ephesians 6 gives us a threefold instruction for successful parenting. First are children, *one category.* Every offspring still at home is under the guidance and discipline of the home. Age, ability, etc.—nothing exceeds the limits of this jurisdiction. Paul's point is that parenting is not about rights, but about submission. There can be only one authority operating in a home at any given time. That authority is delegated to the parents, beginning with the father. There is no place or need for a new government, for example, a "kidocracy."

A second instruction found in this chapter is parents, *one relationship.* By decree the parents are responsible for godly order in their home.

A third instruction teaches children to obey, *one command.* This is the only means to arrive at *honor.* Children must always honor their parents, but while at home, they are also obligated to obey. The chapter goes on to explain that this is *right;* all else is unacceptable and is sin.

Training is necessary to accomplish this goal. Parents are to bring up their children "in the nurture and admonition of the Lord." They are to employ both nurture (reason) and admonition (discipline) to get God's Word and way into their children's hearts. A simple schematic of the human body shows that both the head and the rump are equal distances from the heart, implying, of course, that parents are to train from both directions (down and/or up).

Parenting is a serious matter in the pastor's home. If he fails to rule his own house well, the Scriptures tell us, he forfeits his right to rule the house of God. The only sure way to produce right results is to use right tactics, and these are loving relationships and true respect. Children need to <u>feel</u> and <u>see</u> their parents' love (hugging them and letting them see Dad and Mom hug).

Transparency and a ready willingness to operate in forgiveness build trust, which in turn builds faith; having children full of faith is what God expects from us and what this world needs and is waiting to see.

92. How to Stay Sexually Accountable

The irony of our culture is the flagrant practice of public promiscuity on the one hand and the secrecy that shrouds personal sexuality on the other. The Internet has brought the two evils together by affording private access to unlimited pornography. The fall of ministry into sexual deviation resulting from Internet porn sites is alarming. Case after case of fornication, molestation, and perversion has decimated many gifted and would-do-well ministers of the Gospel, resulting in wasted witnesses and wounded families.

Second on the list of sexual deviation is the formation of illicit relationships resulting from staff positions. When either one or both staff members (male and female) are not bonded in their intimate marriage relationships and/or the marriage covenant is not being honored because of selfish whims, the daily rapport and commonality of vision will fabricate an environment that is open to infatuation. If the husband and wife team is not lovingly accountable, trouble can set in and happen before it is noticed by others—and then it is usually too late.

Third in the list of sexual misdeeds is irresponsible counseling. When a man and a woman spend too much time alone, their ability to avoid *transference* (the counselee transfers her loneliness and need for covering to the counselor) and *countertransference* (the counselor responds to the obvious needs of the counselee) is weakened. The one factor that most pastors fail to realize is the entity of *authority.* Women gravitate to authority (in this case, the office of the pastor). How many times have you noticed that a young, pretty secretary and an older, bald-headed, potbellied pastor fall into an affair? It is not sex appeal that draws her to him, but his authority.

You may feel safe in the midst of this moral storm, but it is not wise to tempt the tempter. The only truly safe place is found with your wife, where you and she have developed a truly transparent relationship. This means she can and does ask you, eyeball to eyeball, "How is it going? What are you doing?" Just talking to or confiding in a minister friend can deal only with the transparency aspect, but it does not and cannot provide the practical solution to any potential problem. Only the wife can do both and do so in private. Test: If you are not presently transparent about finances, diet, and dreams, you are <u>not</u> transparent with your intimate life. Why stay married to a *stranger?* Chances are today that you will not!

93. Be a Man of Your Word

Every man of God knows not to lie, but not all have the ethical resolve to follow truth. Truth is impeccable. It is without compromise, regardless of circumstances. Yet many pastors allow what they promise to fall into the category of untruth because they lack the ethical conviction that truth is not variable, under any circumstance. There are at least three areas in which pastors who believe in the truth find themselves compromising: cluttered calendars, broken promises, and selfish interest.

Busyness is the fruit of success, not an excuse for wrong calendaring. The appointment calendar is much like a fat man eating junk food: irresponsible intake guarantees excess pounds and delayed problems. The sole purpose of a visual calendar (there is *no* accurate mental calendar) is to afford accuracy and honesty in scheduling appointments. Once an appointment is agreed upon, it has sole priority for that time slot. Any change must first be considered by both parties involved. Upgrading a calendared appointment solely for your advancement (a better opportunity) is tantamount to a lie. The calendar is a tool for ministerial stewardship, with the sole purpose of maintaining the best and most orderly use of your time.

The sign of *insincerity* is a broken promise (word). As a minister of the Lord, your simple statement of intention is really a promise to your family, your congregation, and your city. A hasty, people-pleasing agreement to anything without the courteous consideration to the worth of those who are speaking is what the world knows as a *political promise,* a lie based upon the expediency of the moment and the weakness of your character.

The more under your authority the person (people) is, the greater the weight of your word (promise)—first to your family, secondly to your congregation, and finally to those in your community. Strangely, many pastors have reversed this priority structure, which can only result in a loss of credibility. It is amazing how many children have to love a "pastor-daddy," whose personal word has become meaningless to them. It should not be surprising when they grow up that they lump all his words (home and pulpit) into the void of broken promises.

Selfishness in any environment is sin, but nowhere is it more evident than when a pastor leaves the truth for his own interest. For example, tardiness is generally a breach of your word predicated upon selfishness; you agreed to meet someone at a certain time, and because of your lack of discipline, personal distraction, or pride (getting ready for the meeting), you broke your word by being late. Failing to show up for an appointment, neglecting to supply something, or failing to perform a certain task is a breach of your word predicated upon selfishness. In life, you can pretty much do as you please, except when you have given your word. Your *word* always takes a righteous precedent over your whims. There is no scriptural validation for selfishness to mock or ignore truth.

94. How to Avoid Burnout in Ministry

Too much work causes weariness, not burnout. Too little time off causes dullness and inefficiency, not burnout. Burnout is caused by useless busyness resulting from lack of vision. If you are compelled by the Spirit to accomplish a task, sufficient grace is present to keep you going, no matter what does or does not transpire.

Burnout appears when you attempt to do what you are not called to do, or you fail to subscribe to God's *order* in doing it (e.g., a wrong strategy, no Sabbath rest, no living in the peace of God, or misplaced priorities.) If you are called to pastor, you have grace to pastor. God does not make logistical errors or personnel mistakes. Furthermore, God never calls you to anything without giving you a vision (Abraham, David, and Paul). God never gives an assignment then fails to provide a strategy to see it accomplished (Noah, Jesus). God underwrites His will with the well-planned rules of life contained in His Word.

All burnout can be contributed to overload. When you overload a truck, the brakes, transmission, and even the engine begin to have unreasonable wear and tear; because their design is being neglected, burnout is inevitable.

If your love for God ceases to make your calling absolutely exciting and it is not your perennial motive in serving, you are missing something. The power of godly love is easily seen, as Jesus never once succumbed to temptation, because of His love for us. Imagine the pressure that generated for Him!

Stress, not the hardness of your assignment, is the chief ingredient that causes burnout. Stress begins with a wrong understanding of who you are and what you have been called to do. Stress is defined by your trying to do or be what only God can do or be, or by your assuming God will do what He has told you to do or be. God answers prayer. We pray and stand in faith. When the two roles are confused, it causes stress, and stress culminates in burnout.

The antidote for burnout is a daily, loving relationship with our Father God that culminates in peace and obedience. Our service to God is the product of our love for Him; like "wet" and "water," they are unceasingly and effortlessly one and the same.

95. Why You Must Properly Keep Records of Your Preaching

No one builds a building and then throws away the plans, for inevitably they will be needed again and again as remodeling and renovation are needed. So it is with your preaching. A sermon is not just a passing moment, but also a link in your spiritual chain. It is wise stewardship to keep complete and detailed information about all your sermonizing.

Some pastors make very few notes, and I have preached from a brief outline written on a napkin at some restaurant a short time before preaching; however, this is the exception and not the rule (this can be done successfully only when you can preach from the overflow). Ninety-nine percent of the time, you should plan for and take adequate time for prayer, meditation, and sermon construction.

Keeping records of your sermons and preaching has many advantages, and once a system (computer programs do it well) is established, it only requires a brief time to make a record of your preaching, chronologically and topically.

When a sermon is completed, you should have a permanent record of your study results, as well as the finished sermon itself. During study time, I make many more notes than can comfortably and contextually be incorporated into the sermon itself. These need to be saved and filed for future review, revision, and use. Exegeses, expository notes, facts, illustrations, and information pertaining to that text are always ready for use the next time or again and again; like with good reference books, you don't throw your books away when you are through using them for that sermon!

The sermon, whether notes, outline, or manuscript, is your response to the Holy Spirit's anointing, and if it is worth saying once, it is worth keeping for reference or repeating (if God has given you anointed insight that blesses your people, He certainly will bless it each time He calls it forth). A carpenter does not labor all day long on the framing of the house and at the end of the day burn it down, only to start all over again the next day. Keep every message, series of messages, devotionals, media scripts, and all other messages in a topical file so they can be readily accessible, just like the books in your library.

It will do you well to keep a chronological filing system of all your sermons. I have a record of every message I have delivered, no matter where or when. This will allow you to review your preaching content and let you see where you may not be preaching the "full Gospel." You will be amazed at how limited your topical and doctrinal preaching has been. Everyone has his favorite subjects, and without written proof, you will not believe what you are preaching until you are challenged in this area. I use a complete systematic listing of doctrine to guide my sermonizing. As a pastor, you must truly obey Jesus' command, to feed His sheep. In one year's time, you will be able to see the true scope of your "feeding."

Know accurately what, when, and how often you preach; then use these facts to round out your preaching content and frequency. This will help keep you on track to bring your congregation into a new level of understanding, maturity, and service.

96. Keeping Everything in Balance

The Bible makes frequent mention of the practice of moderation, implying that excess of anything in this world opens the door to sin. This is so with diet, time, meditation, emotion, or doctrine, to name just a few areas. This truth of balance has been so helpful in my life that I developed our Ministers Training Institute logo as a set of balance scales with the letters *WO* on one scale platform and the letters *RD* on the other: "The WORD in balance."

Here is how it works: Jesus is Lord. His life on the earth is our very example (pattern) for keeping things in proper balance. What you have to do is to lay each aspect of your life over the pattern (the Word) and candidly observe the comparison. This takes courage; yet, the harder task awaits you: to conform that area of your life to His *pattern.*

When you do this doctrinally, you keep yourself from *heresy.* Heresy is placing one Bible truth ahead of the other biblical truths. To maintain balance, you search the Scriptures and find the balance. Balance is not the opposite of the principle, but what the Bible decrees as the balance to that principle. For example, the balance of faith is not unbelief or even somewhere in the middle. The balance to faith is love (Galatians 5:6). Balance is only necessary with the immanent aspects of God—not the transcendent aspects, such as God *is* truth, because there is no balance to truth.

Balance is easily discerned in the natural, such as in diet, hygiene, work, and time, but it is not always easy to keep (that is why you are out of balance to begin with). On the other hand, balance is not so easily grasped in the areas of the soul, the emotions, the mind, and the will. The way to keep your soul in balance is to keep its parts balanced with the other aspects of the soul. The mind and will always keep emotions in balance, just as the emotions and will guard the mind ("love your enemies").

Much of the time, your balance in life must come from others. The church is a community of persons that are in covenant with one another and serve *together,* as Paul describes the parts of the body needing one another. The closer the person is to you, the greater the opportunity and ability he has to do it. Marriage is designed through gender and covenant love to maintain balance in your life.

97. Your Place in the Community

Every pastor is different in leadership gifting and emotional makeup. The size of your town and the general acceptance of your faith (denominational reference) can also make a difference in your entry into community life as a professional religionist (the secular viewpoint). With these factors in mind, your involvement and acceptance in the community will be more successful if you acknowledge several principles.

Rather than fight the usual apathy and/or politics of the average city's pastors' fellowship, seek out those with whom you can have influence according to vision, hunger for God, and community patriotism. There will be those in your city who have or desire to have your vision of building the kingdom of God rather than just a local congregation. These brethren will stimulate your growth, as you in turn cause them to stretch their ministries in serving God and reaching lost souls.

Some ministers are truly professionals and really do not have a call from God into ministry; they have no real hunger for righteousness, and you will be as uncomfortable trying to relate to them as you would be trying to relate to a women's garden society. Just be warm and friendly, and let your light shine consistently.

There will be those ministers in the community who have a gifting and drive to see the community as a whole advance, morally and spiritually. Many of these men will have political ability and vision. They will either lead or assist you in reformation projects, ranging from helping community schools to guiding the local legislature. Each man of God has a certain responsibility to "stand his watch" in civic affairs in the community in which he ministers.

One goal worthy of consideration is to build an alliance of fellow ministers in your town and use your leadership to assist them in fruitful ministry and healthy peer relationships. Every minister has needs, and many ministers are open to receiving fellowship and affirmation to their calls and ministries. They may well need confirmation and information about the Holy Spirit's plan for church government and local church affairs (despite the group to which they belong). You may feel inferior as to age, experience, or longevity in the ministry, but you have an edge on what God is doing now. Besides, the experience of moving into leadership is valuable, and too, a good follower is always worth his weight in gold.

98. Practicing Humility

The one characteristic of Jesus' earthly ministry that stands out to all who would observe His life as written in the New Testament is His humility. Philippians 2 begins this awesome picture of humility, telling us that the Son of God took on the role of a slave, a slave that was destined to die on a cross. His every teaching hallmarks His humility in that it is laced with compassion for every class of man, preference of others, and His longsuffering and patience shown to everyone who comes to Him. As you can see, humility is a fine blend of all the fruit of the Spirit.

Nothing is clearer or more self-evident than the reality of your personal inadequacy and your "holiness in part" as you struggle with humility. Most of us fail in this endeavor to practice humility because we attempt to be "humble in part." Being or trying to be humble in part is like a chicken trying to lay half an egg.

When you try to abase yourself as did John the Baptist (he did successfully), the attempt turns out like a poorly told joke, that is, a waste of breath. Then again, when you attempt to serve with boldness, the result is like brushing your teeth with a broom: overkill. Then when you try to speak meekly, everyone misses your message; or when you attempt to exhort and encourage, it comes across like a bass drum at a flute recital.

Humility is not a demonstration of self-flagellation, nor is it an Oscar-winning act. Humility is the honest perception of one's self and of others. When I can truly see my *real* self and honestly compare it to Jesus, I am halfway home. Then when I can with love and appreciation honestly evaluate you and your giftings, I will score a run and am walking in humility.

If I am a better piano player than you, it is false humility (pride) to say (because I don't believe it) that you play better than I do. On the other hand, if you can play the piano better than I can, I rejoice in your gifting and am not led to despair or jealousy. Admitting and agreeing on the truth of the matter is true humility, and it affords a tremendous witness and victory.

99. On Giving and Taking Credit

Proverbs 27:2 reminds you to let another praise you and do not do it yourself. There is hardly anything in this life that edifies more than to receive praise. But like honey, too much of it will make you ill.

The pastor will keep a great morale among his people if he will use this vital tool with wisdom and timely discretion. The rules are simple:

> Do it in truth. Nothing shreds credibility faster than false praise.
>
> Do it alone, and confirm it publicly. The largeness of the deed will determine the loudness of the praise.
>
> Do it quickly. A word of praise that is delayed is like kissing a corpse: it doesn't help him a bit!

Every person has need of recognition for some good work; in other words, he needs praise. A pastor who stays sensitive to this will have the same results as a mother who gives vitamins to her family, and the results will be the same as a well-prepared dessert after a meal.

Taking undue credit, on the other hand, is like stealing

money instead of working for it. Like garlic in a roast, it tastes good going down, but the aftereffects are offensive to everyone around. The great need to be accepted or noticed is so overwhelming to many people, especially leaders, that they make the devastating error of trying to force their opinions upon people instead of letting the Holy Spirit discover their ability to others.

Leadership is more persuasive to men when it is discovered; King Saul, with all his faults, really did it right when he was "found among the stuff" as Samuel made public announcement of Israel's new king. One thing is certain: Those who do not now see your leadership will not be any more impressed with it after *you* tell them about it.

Taking credit for someone else's work or thought is something else; this is plagiarizing. This is a sin committed by many in the ministry, the taking of credit for something you did not originally say, write, or do. The honest thing is to always give credit, specifically if you know the person's name. Generally, if it is not your work, it is so easy to say, "Someone said. . ." Obviously, if the statement or act is renowned or so generally known that no one could mistake you for inventing the word or situation, you are excused from giving credit, although for you to mention the person's name may make your statement or story more profound.

Taking or giving credit is an ego issue, and therein lies the danger. You should not take part in tempting your brother with "too much honey," nor should you toot your own horn. And never should you steal someone else's words, wisdom, or deeds.

100. Make Every Service an Evangelistic Opportunity

Every time you are the "governor" of a service or have (you should) requested permission from the one who is in charge, give an invitation to the lost to get saved. Your ministry is too short to ever neglect your primary purpose: bringing the lost to Christ. To fail here is as irresponsible as it would be for you to cook a five-course meal for your guests, seat them at your table, and then refuse to serve the food.

Evangelism should not be a special project in your ministry or done during special services. That would be just like living in a house with no bedroom or kitchen; it would be only half a house. When I pastored, I did not receive an offering in every service held at the church (I surely would have liked to), but as time went on, I never conducted a service where I did not give an invitation to receive Christ as Lord and Savior. Even at weddings, I asked the couple getting married for permission to extend an invitation, and I always included the plan of salvation. Funerals are an excellent time to extend an invitation to the lost; you will always have a good response to the Gospel at the service and as you speak to family members later that day.

Give an evangelistic invitation at <u>every</u> service held at your local church. Even if the teaching is on another subject or is just instruction to believers, first give an invitation for the lost to accept Christ, and then follow with an invitation to respond to the teaching of the hour. The lost are just going to sit through the appeal to the church anyway, so get them to respond first. While they are being briefed in a special prayer room, continue with the rest of the invitation.

One word about inviting people to respond to the preached/taught Word of God: Always give warm, clear instructions as to what it means to be lost and how one is saved. Proceed by directing (telling them) how to follow through on their decisions. Present them with a timed opportunity (30 to 60 seconds stops any emotional misuse of time). Always speak authoritatively (warmly and expectantly); remember that people welcome and will respond very easily to clear guidance when they are in a public situation. The point is not for you to be coercive, but for you to take every offensive strategy against the devil as he attempts to dissuade the potential converts.

101. Keeping Your Testimony Fresh and Alive

Every believer *has* a testimony of his conversion to Jesus Christ. The longer you live in Christ, the more firm and sure it becomes. More than a love story, your testimony is exciting and soul-stirring to believers and nonbelievers alike. The reason it is so effective lies in the fact that your testimony of conversion is so real and meaningful to you.

Even when preaching, your deep conviction of a pet doctrine is not as forceful in persuading people as is your testimony of conversion. Your testimony is so personal—it is *you*—and people realize this instantly and receive it, just like a jury listens to a sworn-in witness in a courtroom. Therefore, you should have your testimony ready to deliver in any and every situation. I can give my testimony in just a minute or two to someone on the street, or I can take an hour to share it before an assembly, especially men.

Your testimony has several powerful effects. One effect of giving your testimony is that it edifies you. It keeps the most important spiritual event in your life alive, fresh, and meaningful. It will "kick start" your day. It will always keep you encouraged, even when the rest of your ministry seems to be down. It will keep you from straying into sin. It will be a light to your feet when discouragement tries to muscle in on your life. It provides a measuring stick for you and all who know you to measure what God did for you against how you are doing now!

Your testimony will inspire people to be saved more quickly than any sermon you can preach, because you were not only a witness to this momentous moment, but also your obvious and excited joy over the grace of God extended to you will be evident. There is nothing more effective in keeping you close to the cross as your experience when it happened. Like true love, it grows more meaningful and sweeter the longer you live.

My conversion was graphic and soul-stirring. Others may have been raised in church all their lives and gotten saved as children during a revival service; to them, their salvation experience may seem bland compared to others. If this is you, do not let the enemy rob you. The powerful work of the Holy Spirit to move you to conviction when every religious demon was pacifying you with your "goodness" is very much a battle. Which is easier: to raise the *dead* (you in your religious slumber) or to deliver a demoniac (an obstinate and wild sinner)? Of course, with God all things are possible. In every case of conversion, His grace is unspeakable. Keep your testimony active; it's really your *best* sermon. This has been my *testimony* for over fifty years.

CPSIA information can be obtained at www.ICGtesting.com
Printed in the USA
LVOW07s1138270814

401103LV00001B/51/A

9 781594 679018